The Christian Vision:
MAN IN SOCIETY

ON THE COVER

God infuses Adam with life in Michaelangelo's *The Creation of Adam*, the central fresco of the cycle on the vault of the Sistine Chapel in the Vatican, Rome.

The Christian Vision:
MAN IN SOCIETY

Edited by Lynne Morris

The Hillsdale College Press
Hillsdale, Michigan 49242

Hillsdale College Press

Books by George Roche; the *Champions of Freedom* series from the Ludwig von Mises Lecture Series on economic policy; *The Essential Imprimis* collection; the CCA-Shavano video and cassette tapes; and the easy-to-read, humorous *Alternatives* program materials to explain the economic facts of life, are all available from the HILLSDALE COLLEGE PRESS, directed by Peter McCarty.

THE CHRISTIAN VISION: MAN IN SOCIETY
© 1984 by Hillsdale College Press
Hillsdale, Michigan 49242

Printed in the United States of America

First Printing 1984
Library of Congress Catalog Card Number: 84-80770
ISBN 0-916308-99-5

Acknowledgments

Special thanks to the following individuals whose valuable help made this book possible: Thomas Burke, Pat DuBois, Carl F. H. Henry, James Juroe, Mark Michaelsen, and Nancy Steward, of Hillsdale College.

Contents

Foreword

The book you hold in your hands represents the realization of an educational vision we have long cherished here at Hillsdale: the establishment of a formal Christian Studies program within our liberal arts curriculum.

The idea for such a program originated in the late 1970s when the estimable scholar Russell Kirk graced our campus as a visiting professor of history and English. Dr. Kirk's proposal for the formation of the program was issued May 20, 1978 and included the signatures of Thomas Howard and Gerhart Niemeyer—contributors to this volume—as well as Sheldon Smith and James Hitchcock.

After six years of planning, the Christian Studies Program is finally a reality. The multidisciplinary curriculum includes course offerings in Hillsdale's religion, English, history and political science departments, leading to an academic minor in Christian Studies. We look forward to the establishment of a major.

Hillsdale is blessed with the presence of Carl F. H. Henry as Distinguished Visiting Professor of Christian Studies. This eminent theologian and servant of the Lord has inspired the first year of our program. Professor Henry and his colleague, the Rev. Thomas Burke, ably teach the Christian Studies courses in religion, as do Drs. John Willson and Warren Treadgold in history and Drs. James Juroe and Benjamin Alexander in English.

We celebrate the inception of Hillsdale's newest academic program in typical Hillsdale fashion. The Center for Constructive Alternatives began the 1983–84 school year with a week-long seminar whose distinguished participants' remarks you will find in this volume. The intellectual and spiritual vitality which marked that seminar indicates that Hillsdale has begun to shape something all too rare on college campuses today — an academic curriculum that allows the student to explore deeply his faith and his relationship to God within a context of a rigorous liberal arts education.

Our program's goal is to enable an interested student to recognize and appreciate the influence of Christianity upon Western culture and to understand his rights and responsibilities within the culture; to equip the student for constructive evaluation of his own moral and spiritual values; and to inform the student about Christian teachings concerning God and man's relationship to him.

The new program has had an immediate impact on other departments too, as philosophy, music and theatre courses shape themselves to complement Christian Studies, much as growing plants will turn to face the light.

The program is nondenominational. The faculty represent most of the major Christian faiths, and guest lecturers include representatives of non-Christian traditions as well. This is in keeping with the spirit of free inquiry with which the 1844 Baptist founders chartered the school.

Our future rests on the shoulders of the next generation of leaders. In an educational setting as exciting, inspiring, and challenging as the essays in this volume, Hillsdale is striving to expose students to the truths of the past in combination with the academic and scientific breakthroughs of the present.

Through broad outreach programs like the Hillsdale College Press, Hillsdale is also sharing the spirit and the best of the thought generated through our campus programs and special events with readers around the world.

The essays that follow, then, describe something quite remarkable in this utilitarian and reductionist era: a vision realized. I commend them to your thoughtful reading.

George Roche
Hillsdale, Michigan

Introduction

"Where there is no vision, the people perish." Prov. 29:18

As a self-conscious being, man reflects not only on the world within him and the world about him, but also upon his ultimate context, the world "above" him. Despite recent denials that talk of this larger context is meaningful, this dimension must not be ignored. The surreptitious cloaking of metaphysical concepts in current "anti-metaphysical" philosophies demonstrates the need for critical counterbalance. As an alternative, the Christian vision deserves serious and informed exploration and evaluation. No other world view has so encompassed all aspects of reality nor has had such dramatically influential effects upon man's understanding of his world and the whole of human life.

To speak of *the* Christian vision may seem somewhat presumptuous. There are, after all, numerous systems of Christian thought, some incompatible with one another and, on the surface, at times even at cross purposes. Yet these attempts to explicate the Christian faith and to draw out its implications derive from a core of commonly held beliefs and assumptions about God and the world. Regardless of differences on the extent of original sin, the nature of justification, the relationship of nature and grace, etc., all truly Christian intellectual endeavor is founded on the assumption of an Eternal, Triune God who has created the world, and who by means of the God-man Jesus Christ, his "only begotten" Son, is in the process of redeeming a fallen mankind from the ravages of human rebellion against divine prerogatives. Moreover, it is a fundamental assumption that our knowledge of this God and his redemptive activity is grounded in the Old and New Testaments.

The absence from most all academic institutions — even some church-related schools — of a coherent curriculum structured around these basal Christian convictions has led Hillsdale College to add a program of Christian studies to its curriculum. Approaching the liberal arts from this theological perspective, the program is neither sectarian nor ecumenical. It neither limits itself to the viewpoint of one particular branch of Christianity nor reduces beliefs to a lowest common denominator. Involving representatives as diverse as conservative Roman Catholics on the one hand and evangelical Baptists on the other, it presents a study of the arts, literature, philosophy, and history in the context of fundamental Christian attitudes and convictions. It is not, however, merely a duplication of a traditional Christian college curriculum. In the context of a secular college campus, it seeks to present students with a Christian vision of the world as a viable intellectual alternative, and to integrate that viewpoint into their total educational program. Its setting, diversity, and structure make it a unique and imaginative educational experiment.

Hillsdale's Christian Studies Program does not aim at simply conserving and informing, but also at developing a vision of reality that integrates Christian theism with modern disciplines in constructive ways that will significantly contribute to our understanding of reality. It presents a perspective on the world, a "meaning context," which surpasses secular and Marxist alternatives in beauty, goodness, and truth. Such a vision was responsible for the dramatic development of Western culture on the ruins of the drained and desiccated Greco-Roman civilization of antiquity. This vision, spawned in pre-Hellenistic Palestine and enriched by the intellectual achievements of the ancient Mediterranean civilizations, blossomed into a culture which has culminated in the greatest political, economic, cultural, and scientific achievements ever attained.

The vision of the world in which classical, orthodox Christianity has been nurtured and to which it has given expression is the only viable alternative to the shallowness of modern humanism and the radical absurdity of contemporary Marxism. But that vision needs contemporary expression in light of present circumstances, and forceful argumentation in modalities attuned to men and women raised in a culture devoid of intellectual or moral depth. Moreover, it needs to be unfolded in reference to modern man's most flagrant error, his fundamental misunderstanding of his own nature and his own place in nature. It is here that Christianity can be both corrective and constructive, for it views man as created in the image of God and therein receiving from his Creator a transcendent purpose which lends each human person and human history generally a dignity, value, and meaning which far surpass that envisioned by any other world view, ancient or modern.

Convinced of this, the present volume attempts to give expression to this vision of human existence as it impinges upon our understanding of humanness and human intellectual and cultural endeavor.

These papers were delivered at a seminar of the Center for Constructive Alternatives on the Hillsdale College campus in September, 1983. The week-long convocation focused on the topic, "*Imago Dei*: A Christian Vision of Man," and sought to relate the fundamental Christian vision of man as created in the image of God to some of the central areas of human action. Education, psychology, culture, science, and law were among the topics selected. The papers included in this volume were delivered as key addresses to stimulate thought and discussion.

In the first paper, Dr. Carl F. H. Henry analyzes the drastic consequences of modern secularity in the academic world. He notes a current resurgence of theism, one that may presage a return to an intellectual foundation capable of sustaining the achievements of Western society. Henry argues that modern secularism, characterized by "*diffuse* dependency, *total* transiency, *radical* relativity and *absolute* autonomy," has undermined the coherence of the Western intellectual tradition, deprived it of rational criteria by which to judge human life and society, and has staved off collapse of the human spirit only by illogically maintaining values founded in the Christian tradition, but having only an arbitrary connection with secularism itself.

Christianity and culture have always had an uneasy relationship, and in our second selection, Dr. Thomas Howard examines the tension which exists perennially between Athens and Jerusalem. He argues that while culture is a good, even a grand thing, it is not a means of salvation, and only if its limitations are recognized and its aims properly circumscribed can the Christian keep culture from becoming a minor deity and distorting, or even destroying, the Christian faith.

The noted philosopher of science, Dr. Stanley Jaki, discusses the humanness of the scientific enterprise and the various ways in which this humanness influences how science is done and what is done with science. He brings his extensive knowledge of the history of science to lead up to a discussion of the nature of the cosmos as science presently envisions it. The implications of our current knowledge are then used to develop an outline for a contemporary cosmological argument for the existence of God. His penetrating analysis of the nature of the relationship among science, cosmology, and theology challenges commonly held assumptions about the neutrality, or worse, the irrelevance of theology to the modern queen of academics.

The universal scope of religion's claims upon its adherents always eventuates in the need to develop a theory of church-state relations, especially the scope and limits of the individual believer's responsibilities to each. This entails the need for a Christian view of the political order which demarcates the place of the state in ordering the life of society. But one can only create such a view in the context and on the basis of an anthropology and a philosophy of history.

Dr. Gerhart Niemeyer presents a stimulating paper which analyzes the seminal thought of St. Augustine in its historical and philosophical context in order to demonstrate the importance of a balanced ontology and ethics if one is to avoid the dangers of totalitarianism. Niemeyer show how Augustine's ontology, grounded in the biblical view of creation *ex nihilo*, provides the intellectual framework from which he develops a theory of adversity and an ethic on which he then builds his thought about the political order and its place in human history. Niemeyer argues that while Augustine actually does not have a political philosophy *per se*, he does establish parameters which political theory today can disregard only to its own peril. Rich in the history of philosophical anthropology and ethics, Niemeyer's paper provides fertile soil for stimulating discussion on ontology, ethics, philosophy of religion, and philosophy of law as well as political philosophy.

A Christian vision of man as created in the image of God must influence one's view of personality and, consequently, inform one's psychology, both conceptually and practically. In the fifth essay, Dr. Paul Vitz gives a concrete example of how a Christian view of mankind can profitably influence and enrich modern psychological theory and practice, providing values and conceptual paradigms superior to any derivable from a purely secular psychology. At the basis of an adequate concept of personality, he argues, lies the biblical view of covenant, and only when seen in that context can our view of man be such that our psychological practice will address the person as he truly is. Vitz contends that secular psychology, by leaving religion out of its view of man, omits some of the basic components of a satisfactory psychological theory and so distorts other components that their employment often becomes more harmful than helpful. Vitz does not merely criticize the failures and shortcomings of modern psychology, however, but presents his critique in the context of an outline for a Christian theory of personality.

Dr. James Packer's offering provides a clear, precise, and beautifully organized presentation of the theological view of man. In the framework of what he calls a "Christian Humanism," Packer deals with the central issues, from a Christian point of view, regarding man, his fallenness, and God's gracious, redemptive action in Jesus Christ. His exploration and development of these central concerns provide a perspicacious answer to the pressing intellectual and existential questions confronting modern man: "Who am I? Why am I (are we) here? What can I hope for?" The relevance of Christian faith and the superiority of its answer to these essential issues is forcefully conveyed by Packer's article.

Lastly, my contribution attempts to explain and defend the intellectual integrity of Hillsdale's Christian Studies Program, and thereby to provide a rationale for other similar programs. First, the nature and aims of Hillsdale's program are developed, and then obvious charges of non-objectivity and compromises of academic freedom are examined and answered. Such accusations, it is argued, stem from a misunderstanding of both collegiate education and intellectual objectivity. Indeed, a case is constructed for an inherent compatibility between the liberal arts and a Christian world view.

The specificity and pertinence of these papers, the centrality of the issues they address, and their timeliness and importance to crucial concerns on the contemporary scene, make them ideal reading for classes in religion, philosophy, sociology, and history. Their originality and insight provide an excellent starting point from which discussion and debate can spring. Our intellectual, cultural, economic, and political accomplishments do little but prolong and mollify an evanescent existence with but transient and self-directed activity unless achieved for ends transcending the purely finite. Isolated from any comprehensive and purposeful vision of human life, man's estrangement from his world and his fellow humans becomes oppressively burdensome and his life an unbearable drudgery. A vision is needed which will lift human existence from the aimless cycle of a self-perpetuating nature to the transcendent and eternal arena of the Living, Speaking, Acting, and Purposing God who created man in His own image. We hope this collection of essays will be a significant contribution to vital, contemporary expressions of the Christian vision of man.

Dr. Thomas Burke
Hillsdale College
March 25, 1984

The Crisis of Modern Learning

Carl F. H. Henry

Dr. Carl F. H. Henry, Lecturer-at-Large for World Vision International, is currently Distinguished Visiting Professor of Christian Studies, Hillsdale College. Dr. Henry received his undergraduate degree from Wheaton College and earned doctorates from Boston University and the Northern Baptist Theological Seminary. He has been professor of theology at both Northern and Eastern Baptist Seminaries and at Fuller Seminary. He has held numerous visiting professorships at colleges and universities throughout the world. Past president of the American Theological Society, he was founding editor of the influential evangelical fortnightly, *Christianity Today*, which he edited for 12 years. The author of hundreds of articles, 28 books, and editor of 11 more, Dr. Henry has just completed his massive six-volume analysis of contemporary theological systems and thought, *God, Revelation and Authority*.

The most sudden and sweeping upheaval in beliefs and values has taken place in this century. No generation in the history of human thought has seen such swift and radical inversion of ideas and ideals as in our lifetime.

At the outset of this century the instructional program of the great Western universities frequently referred to the God of the Bible, the living self-revealing God. Courses in moral philosophy gave prominence to the Ten Commandments and to the Sermon on the Mount, and presented Jesus of Nazareth as the perfect example of morality. Studies in social philosophy stressed that for history to attain a utopian future some change in man's inner disposition or character is necessary, if not because of original sin (which was increasingly questioned on

1

evolutionary assumptions) then at least because of man's supposed inheritance of brute propensities and animal instincts.

By the late 1920s a striking shift of perspective had prevailed. References to deity no longer focused on the God of Abraham, Isaac and Jacob, the self-revelatory God of biblical theism, but rather on an anonymous God-in-general, a John Doe god. God was now inferred from the not-God. Philosophers of religion argued from the existence of the cosmos to a divine Cause, and/or from the design of nature or pattern of history to a divine Designer, and/or from human conscience to a divine Lawgiver, or from the mind of man to an Absolute Reason. Instead of the One God there emerged varieties of gods, both infinite and finite, personal and impersonal, even growing gods. Naturalists, meanwhile, dismissed God entirely except as but a convenient symbol for man's supreme social or private values. Little agreement survived over the nature of deity even among philosophers who considered metaphysics their special province. Faced by this vanishing theoretical consensus, American educators abandoned the concept of God as the integrating factor in modern university learning.

Instead of God, shared moral values became the cohesive force in liberal arts studies. This emphasis on ethical norms was not, however, associated with biblical imperatives and divinely revealed commandments. The study of morals was increasingly pursued independently of theological concerns, although some campuses nonetheless scheduled annual "spiritual emphasis" weeks, not unmindful of promotional and funding benefits amid waning if not already severed denominational ties. Man's distinctive nature, it was said, requires a hierarchy of values that in preserving material realities subordinates them to ethical duties; these ethical duties, however, may or may not in turn require spiritual or theological illumination.

The shift of educational perspective concerned not only the vision of God and of moral imperatives, but also the nature of the dawning future and the means of implementing utopia. No longer was an internal change in man's nature or character considered necessary, and especially not the supernatural regeneration of fallen man on which Christian theism insisted. Instead, education, politicization and socialization of the human race were to be the catalysts of a new age. Western learning would be carried to the ends of the earth, democratic ideals would be exported to all the nations, and the realities of human brotherhood in one world would facilitate the triumph of universal peace and justice.

Today much of that kind of thinking is gone.

No significant place remains for God or the gods in the university classroom. Courses in science and in history dismiss deity as irrelevant. Psychology texts usually introduce God only as a psychic aberration. Even some religion departments still rumor the "death of God." Philosophy departments are in the grip of postpositivistic analysis and tend to sidestep supernatural concerns; others disown the supernatural and creatively restructure ultimate reality. Over against most departments where both the God of the Bible and the John Doe god, that is, God-in-general, are shunned as extraneous, the literature department alone seems at least to reflect the great theological concerns in a literary context.

In the absence of unrevisable absolutes, universities vainly expected that common values would nonetheless integrate modern learning. What we actually have is a normless tolerance of diversity, of deviation which is linked with a democratic outlook and often with respect for minorities; moral absolutes are associated only with totalitarian bureaucracies. A relativistic morality given to self-assertion lampoons the truth that tolerance without norms destroys even tolerance and that democracy without norms invites chaos.

Not only have the pluralistic gods and shared moral values become pale ghosts of the campus, but confidence has broken down as well in education and politics as dynamic catalysts of social change. Instead of reliance on orderly means of social change, including respect for law and deference to established conventions, the mood of contemporary social transformers is increasingly open to revolutionary coercion and violence as the preferred alternatives that assure rapid and radical alteration.

Meanwhile education itself succumbs to pressures to curtail the humanities, a course that would even more abridge the already reduced common intellectual experience of students. These pressures come not only from the side of the physical sciences which are now the *sine qua non* of modern learning, but also from the vocational needs of students. They come no less from a sense that academe has lost intellectual excitement and reward. The liberal arts have impoverished themselves by their neglect of enduring spiritual concerns and by their studied exclusion of Judeo-Christian perspective in a radically secular age.

The drift of twentieth-century learning can be succinctly summarized in one statement: instead of recognizing Yahweh as the source and stipulator of truth and the good, contemporary thought reduces all reality to impersonal processes and events, and insists that man himself creatively imposes upon the cosmos and upon history the only values that they will ever bear. This dethronement of God and enthronement of man as lord of the universe, this eclipse of the supernatural and exaggeration of the natural, has precipitated an intellectual and moral crisis that escorts Western civilization despite its brilliant technological achievements ever nearer to anguished collapse and atheistic suffocation.

I

The shaping ideas of contemporary university learning can be readily identified. Its key concepts are dependency, transiency, relativity and autonomy. These terms have always had a proper place in the explanation of man and the world, and all the more so in a generation that knows the space-time universe to be immensely older and immensely larger than even our grandparents suspected. But what distinguishes the modern view is its antitheological and antisupernatural stance. The modern view affirms *diffuse* dependency, *total* transiency, *radical* relativity and *absolute* autonomy.

In affirming the independence of God, classic education denied the comprehensive contingency of all reality: the Creator of the universe has the ground of his being in himself, that is, has *aseity*, whereas the universe in its totality is dependent upon its Maker and is pervasively contingent. The current view, by contrast, depicts all reality as a matrix of contingency; all existence reduces ultimately to nature in some form, that is, to physical processes and events.

Earlier education affirmed, further, the reality of an eternal spiritual and moral world grounded in the supernatural being of God; it denied that reality is completely in the clutch of time. By contrast the current view affirms the transiency of the whole of existence. The biblical conception of an eternal Logos who shaped all worlds humanism considers mythology and without explanatory importance. All that exists, we are told, bears an expiration date; man and beast alike move toward death as their final destiny.

Earlier education affirmed that truth and the good are fixed and final; it denied that right and wrong are culture-relative. The current view, on the other hand, asserts that all ideas and ideals are relative to culture: all ethical imperatives, all philosophical pronouncements, all theological doctrines, are partisan prejudices of the socio-cultural matrix. It rejects outright eternal and revealed truths, divinely given commandments, unrevisable religious doctrines.

Given this emphasis on the culture-relativity of truth, certain other tenets of the current view seem somewhat arbitrary, for example, its confident dogmas of complete contingency and total transiency. The fact is, that a consistent espousal of culture-relativity would lead not to such speculative finalities, but to skepticism, since pervasive dependency and total transiency would be doctrines rooted in our own particular cultural perspective.

But the current view also affirms, and aggressively so, the absolute autonomy of man. Its test of whether modern man has truly "come of age" turns on whether one repudiates all external, objective, and transcendent authority, and affirms instead the ultimacy of personal decision and creative selfhood. Man is considered his own lord in the area of truth and morals; the only values that the cosmos and history will ever bear, in the current view, are those that man himself insinuates into the course of events.

For more than a decade these premises — diffuse dependency, total transiency, radical relativity and absolute autonomy — have dominated the university classroom more influentially than any and all other alternatives. They have become the masked metaphysics, the covert conceptuality of modern liberal learning. Almost every sampling of student reaction to liberal arts studies in the mainstream colleges and universities in the last decade evokes the overwhelming verdict that recent students considered themselves intellectually constrained to shape their world view by these controlling emphases as they authoritatively permeated classroom teaching and discussion. This naturalist outlook notably differs from the atheistic Communist view only in secondary details rather than in basic assumptions. The official teaching of Communism is that nature and history are objectively structured by a pattern of economic determinism, a determinism that assures the ultimate triumph of the proletariat. Free-world naturalism, by contrast, views this claim as pure mythology, and considers nature and history instead to be intrinsically unpatterned. But both perspectives are equally antitheological, both repudiate a divinely given truth and morality, and both reject a supernatural purpose in nature and history. While Communism views the state as the authoritative stipulator of truth and right for the collectivity of mankind, free-world naturalism on the other hand elevates creative individual selfhood.

It is a fact, of course, that the present student generation is less idea-oriented than job-oriented. Some reports estimate the number of seriously intellectual students at only 10 percent. Some improvement is under way as women students aspire to careers in medicine, law and other professions long dominated by men. As other coveted vocational opportunities presuppose academic competence serious students competing for scholarships are once again returning to long-forsaken libraries. Scholars who consciously accept the naturalistic world view are frequently encouraged by their mentors to pursue graduate studies and to become university teachers. Among most students, the pressures of naturalistic theory serve actually to dull the force of the inherited Judeo-Christian view or at very least to postpone individual commitment to its high moral and spiritual demands. The emergence of selfism or a *me*-first outlook on life is resisted most strenuously by that minority of students who, against the winds of modernity, maintain vital ties to orthodox Judaism, Catholicism or evangelical Protestantism. The overall impact of recent liberal arts studies has been to seal off the spiritual world, however, and to concentrate classroom interest on changing space-time tentativities.

II

What specially attracts liberal arts students to naturalism is its emergence in the form of humanism, a philosophic system that adds to the naturalistic agenda a program of social ethics. Humanism emphasizes not only man's duties to his fellow man and to nature, but also certain expectations from his fellow man and from nature. Human beings ought to champion social justice, promote human rights and racial equality and be concerned, we are told, about poverty; they ought, moreover, to preserve natural resources and avoid polluting the cosmos. Humanism emphasizes also certain human expectations from nature, which is assumed somehow to uphold personal worth and security. Although most secularists abandon any expectation of individual immortality, some have assigned their bodies to deep freeze at death in the hope that science in the next century will be able to retrieve them for endless life on earth.

This correlation of a humanist agenda of social ethics with a naturalistic world view has been attacked from right and left as a philosophical monstrosity that defies logical consistency. A system that denies that personality has decisive significance in the origin of the universe and considers personality but an accidental by-product of blind and unthinking forces can hardly affirm that nature specially defers to man or that man is bound by enduring duties. The consistent outcome of naturalistic theory is not a special status for mankind but the essential purposelessness and meaninglessness of human existence. The inconsistency of the humanist is perhaps most apparent in his existential response when he is wronged by a fellow human being. If a humanist professor at New York University were to park his new Jaguar in a parking lot and to discover upon returning that an unknown driver had done massive damage to the side of his car, he would predictably not offer a public eulogy to the latest defector from objective values who, having emerged from ethical adolescence, now considered all ethical imperatives culturally-relative and creative selfhood to be decisive for morality. Far from it. He would, instead, suddenly inherit a vocabulary with eschatological overtones that his naturalistic metaphysics does not logically accommodate.

From the right, that is, from the side of biblical theism, the humanist emphasis on social ethics has long been assailed as a borrowed fragment of the Judeo-Christian heritage which it was unable completely to disavow. Christian theism by contrast affirms not only a program of social ethics; it affirms also an agenda of personal ethics and, moreover, insists that love for God holds priority over love for neighbor and for self. Modern secular philosophy, as D. Elton Trueblood contended, promoted a "cut-flower civilization," one destined to wither because severed from its biblical roots; moreover, it preserved only preferred remnants of the Judeo-Christian moral imperative.

Evangelical criticism of the humanist program was not, however, a powerful intellectual classroom force. Only a minority boldly voiced its claims against the counterpressures of comprehensive naturalism. Evangelicals, moreover, were themselves embarrassed by propagandistic fundamentalist claims that humanists, in view of their atheism and tolerance of deviant lifestyles, were the enemies of morality.

More recently, however, criticism of the illogic of humanism has proceeded increasingly from the left. Radical students who identify themselves with the naturalistic world view have pressed university professors to defend their espousal of "conventional morality" in the realm of social ethics given the controlling tenets on which humanism rests. As Karl Lowith remarks, naturalism provides no real basis for man to feel "at home" amid statistical averages in a universe born of an explosion. One can go further. Naturalism provides no objective basis for moral obligation, no basis for expecting that the cosmos will specially cater to man. The governing principles of comprehensive contingency, total transiency, and radical relativity can accommodate no special meaning and worth for human existence. A cosmos in which personhood emerges only as an oddity and as an accident cannot sustain as its primary value an agenda of man's objective duties to nature or to his fellow beings. The consistent implication of naturalism is that man does not matter and that nature has no special place for personality. Naturalistic evolution can sustain neither the universal nor the permanent dignity of man.

The humanist modification of naturalism to accommodate an agenda of social ethics is evidence enough that while naturalism as a metaphysical system is thinkable, it is not humanly livable. Naturalism dissolves the worth and meaning of human survival. The naturalist postulates one set of ideas theoretically; the humanist adjusts them experientially and existentially to contrary expectations from nature and man.

III

I have noted cardinal assumptions of the modern world view and indicated that humanism modifies the naturalistic mind-set by illogically appending an agenda of social ethics and insisting on the special value of man. The reason for this deviation, however inconsistent with the basic beliefs of naturalism, is not a matter simply of illogic. Nor is this compromise due only to sentimentality, that is, to an inability of humanists, contrary to hard-core naturalists, to divest themselves wholly of inherited Judeo-Christian precepts, although humanism does in fact accommodate fragments of conventional morality that naturalism in principle excludes. What needs specially to be stressed, however, is that the reason humanism adjusts naturalistic beliefs experientially to universal ethical imperatives is that like every other human being the humanist is related to a larger realm of being and life and value, one that he neither creates nor controls. He cannot wholly escape God in his revelation nor wholly suppress the claim of the *imago Dei* upon his psyche. He is informed about inescapable moral obligation far more than the naturalistic theory implies. The New Testament clearly affirms that the Logos of God lights every man (John 1:9) and that the revelation of the Creator penetrates to the very being of even those who would suppress or excise that disclosure (Rom. 1:18 ff., 2:14 f.). Despite his intellectual and moral revolt against the supernatural, fallen man is unable to fully free himself of God's counterclaim upon his mind and conscience.

Secular man vetoes God's claim intellectually and by his own theoretical postulations renders that claim personally powerless. But he does not thereby cancel or destroy that claim, nor can he wholly escape it. His very compromise of the naturalistic world view shows that his theoretical atheism is inadequate to explain the totality of existence. The humanist is torn between contrary demands: while his radically secular theory renders supernatural claims ridiculous and irrelevant, his moral and ontological claims about man and society have no real basis in a naturalistic view but actually link man responsibly to God in his revelation. On a naturalistic basis he cannot consistently mount a persuasive case for ethical imperatives. What stimulates him to moral concern is the inescapable general revelation of God and the ineradicable *imago Dei* which, however sullied by sin, survives in man as the imperishable gift of the Creator.

The humanist perspective, therefore, is nurtured in part by hidden resources. At the crucial point of the nature and destiny of man the humanist forsakes the consistent demands of naturalism and incorporates instead alternatives that only a theistic view can coherently and adequately sustain. The Bible clearly illumines the tension that besets the humanist's refusal to opt either for thoroughgoing naturalism or for thoroughgoing theism. On the one hand the universal general revelation of God, in which the humanist shares, explains his concessions and departures from a consistent naturalistic account of man and the world; on the other, spiritual rebellion or sin explains his theoretical exclusion of the supernatural. The humanist seeks to suppress God's claim but cannot wholly eradicate it. Like all other human beings he stands perpetually related to God in his self-disclosure and cannot totally obscure the *imago Dei* that by creation stamps man with special dignity and worth.

IV

Given the intellectual dominance of naturalism in the contemporary university, one would expect that if ever a student generation were to be wholly lost to a supernatural faith, and especially to the Judeo-Christian heritage with its distinctive revelatory claim, the present collegiate masses would be doomed to that fate. Yet it is one thing to say that on balance the university classroom most influentially promulgates the view that impersonal processes and events comprise the ultimately real world, and quite another to say that atheistic naturalism, whether humanist or nonhumanist, has captured the student mind. While most students, even many who pursue studies in philosophy, delay any serious wrestling of metaphysical concerns, there are tens of thousands in the American evangelical movement whose personal faith in Christ and commitment to Christian theism dates back to high school and university. Their exposure to Judeo-Christian realities came not in connection with classroom studies, but mainly on the margin of formal studies, through association with fellow students whose devotional vitality and moral dedication contrasted notably with the spiritual apathy and ethical permissiveness prevalent on the secular campus.

In large part ecumenical student activity had waned because

of concessions to the speculative climate; doctrinal and evange-
listic concerns were replaced by radical socio-political protest.
Evangelical movements like Inter-Varsity Christian Fellowship,
Campus Crusade for Christ, Young Life and Navigators left
their mark despite contrary academic pressures. Such evangelical efforts were experience-centered, although Inter-Varsity in
America like its British counterpart engaged increasingly in the
publication of books that enlisted the student mind. But even
on mainstream secular campuses scores and then hundreds of
students emerged to witness that they had found the crucified
and risen Christ a living reality and now treasured the Bible as
God's written Word. Like Augustine they declared that the presuppositions of secular philosophy are not necessarily infallible,
and with disarming confidence spoke of supernatural realities
and staked their lives on the eternal verities. Like C. S. Lewis,
they affirmed that one can be *Surprised by Joy* in an intellectual
climate hostile to or oblivious of God and literate only about
space-time relativities. As is well known the Urbana, Illinois,
Inter-Varsity conferences have gathered some 18,000 evangelical collegians. Of these as many as half the participants in one
conference attested that they had ventured a Christian commitment only during the three preceding years. In due course this
tide of evangelical students has swelled enrollments at conservative seminaries, and mainline denominations, faced by declin-
ing missionary volunteers, have looked increasingly to the inter-
denominational student movement for recruits.

To be sure, the evangelical resurgence reflected for some perhaps little more than a semipopular interest in ideas. The elec-
tronic church was led in large part by charismatic personalities
more gifted in inspirational than in theoretical and apologetic
concerns. Religious booksellers capitalized on the conservative
advance by promoting bestseller works dwelling on personal
experience, doctrinal controversy, eschatological speculation
and the like. Evangelists established universities as rivals to
secular institutions.

The Christian day school movement zoomed into high gear,
often depicting public schools as essentially godless and amoral,

even as champions of public schools often depicted private schools as elitist and racist. Newly formed evangelical universities often portrayed the secular campus as essentially atheistic and permissive in perspective, a judgment whose severity went far beyond that of long-established American evangelical colleges for whom the recovery of secular institutions for traditional theistic commitments remained an objective.

In such a climate of extremism secular educators tended to dismiss the growing evangelical movement as an emotion-ridden aberration too intellectually impoverished to endure and regarded humanism as the firmly entrenched and quasi-official philosophy of the secular campus.

There are indications, however, that this verdict seriously misreads the facts. For one thing, the most recent Gallup poll indicates that spiritual interest on the part of university students has not run its course but remains a campus phenomenon. Four in five students consider religious beliefs important, two in five attend religious services weekly, one in three affirm that their religious commitments are deepening rather than weakening. While this religious inquiry takes a variety of turns, and includes an interest in cults like Hare Krishna and the Unification Church as well as in Islam and all branches of the Judeo-Christian movement, evangelical concerns still remain prominently at the center of the movement.

Meanwhile, more and more spokesmen from within the secular universities lament the decline of interest in the humanities, and the attrition of educational core content that increasingly deprives students of a shared academic experience; they also fault the campuses for indifference to the persistent problems of philosophy, among them the reality of God and the objectivity of moral imperatives. As Stephen Muller, president of Johns Hopkins, puts it, the universities may be producing a generation of "highly skilled barbarians."

A further sign of continuing spiritual resurgence is the fact that three recent leaders of the American Philosophical Association, in their presidential addresses, placed the subject of Christian theism once again on the agenda of the society. From

within the APA has emerged a Society of Christian Philosophers which will soon publish a thought journal. The Institute
for Advanced Christian Studies has begun issuing ten paperback texts at junior-college level; written mostly by professors
at Big Ten and other mainline universities, the series gives
Christian perspective on various liberal arts disciplines. Evangelical texts are appearing also in philosophy and theology that
underscore the importance of Christian theism for the intellectual as well as social life of the culture and reach beyond empirical and historical methodology in probing ultimate reality. A
growing confluence of literature by Jewish, Catholic and Protestant scholars is now emerging as well; in a secular society
whose pluralism lacks purpose and whose normless tolerance
invites chaos it is reaffirming the importance of biblical convictions and values. It was Nathan Pusey, former president of
Harvard, who remarked at commencement exercises a generation ago that "the least that can be expected" from a university
graduate is that he or she "pronounce the name of God without
embarrassment."

Modern liberal learning is at a decisive crossroads. In accepting the Templeton Prize for Progress in Religion Aleksandr
Solzhenitsyn put the issue bluntly: "If I were asked today to
formulate as concisely as possible the main cause of the ruinous
Revolution that swallowed up some sixty million of our people," he said, "I could not put it more accurately than to repeat:
'Men have forgotten God; that's why all this has happened'."
This forsaking of God Solzhenitsyn proceeded to identify as
"the principal trait of the entire twentieth century. . . . The
entire twentieth century is being sucked into the vortex of atheism and self-destruction." It is one thing, he observed, that
millions of human beings "have been corrupted and spiritually
devastated by an officially imposed atheism"; it is another,
hardly less disconcerting, that "the tide of secularism . . . has
progressively inundated the West" so that "the concepts of good
and evil have been ridiculed." It "has become embarrassing to
appeal to eternal concepts, embarrassing to state that evil
makes its home in the individual human heart before it enters a

political system," Solzhenitsyn remarked; "the meaning of life in the West has ceased to be seen as anything more lofty than the 'pursuit of happiness'."

Judgment for this eclipse of spiritual realities and for preoccupation with the space-time problematics of nature must fall more severely on us educators than upon our students; indeed, students now often excel their professors in probing the transcendent world. Whether this interest will be permanently shunted to the edge of the classroom is simply another way of asking whether the world of liberal learning is willing to restore academic visibility once again to the priority of God and to ethical imperatives.

At a meeting of the American Association of University Professors shortly after Watergate, some members proposed a resolution condemning the political amorality that precipitated the national scandal. The proposal was quickly withdrawn, however, when someone observed that all major Watergate personalities had attended universities whose faculties are affiliated with A.A.U.P.

If the role of professors does not extend beyond social criticism to involve perpetual vigilance in grappling with and clarifying influential ideas and ideals, are we not accountable, at least in part, for a nation's loss of integrity and moral cohesion?

Is man but a physically upright and mentally clever animal or does he bear the image, however tarnished, of a holy and merciful personal Creator? Are we but complex creatures evolved from matter on an inconsequential planet itself the product of an unconscious collision of blind forces, or is the universe the work of a solicitous Creator who summons us to entrust our well-being and destiny to Him? Does human existence move only toward cessation of life or are there, in fact, transcendent finalities and ultimate destinies in the offing? Contemporary education seems to escape, if not to evade, such issues and in so doing, shortchanges learning by trivializing truth and the good.

While the verdict that intellectuals give on God and the good may not decide the ultimate destiny of contemporary culture, it will nonetheless judge their competence as intellectual and moral analysts to whom are entrusted the fortunes of oncoming generations. When the Roman Empire collapsed in ignominious ruin, it was not the nobles and sages who perpetuated the moral fortunes of the West but rather the scattered people of God who lived according to spiritual and ethical imperatives. What may well be at stake in the crisis of modern learning is not simply the significant survival of society but especially the significant survival of the university. Academia must recover the conviction and promulgation of shared values, of which in the West that of God has been supreme above all. Unless it does so, the fading space-time relativities will by default replace what was once the vision of God and of the good, and will doom man to mistake himself and his neighbor for passing shadows in the night, transient oddities with no future but the grave.

Mere Christianity:
A Focus on Man in Society

Thomas Howard

Dr. Thomas Howard, Professor of English Language and Literature, Gordon College, Wenham, Massachusetts, is best known for his books, *Christ the Tiger, An Antique Drum, Splendor in the Ordinary, Chance or the Dance, Dialogue with a Skeptic, Hallowed Be This House*, and most recently, *The Words of Charles Williams*. A graduate of Wheaton College, Howard received his M.A. from the University of Illinois and his Ph.D. from New York University. Dr. Howard is a frequent guest lecturer at colleges and universities, often directing seminars on the twentieth-century English writer, C. S. Lewis, the subject of his book, *The Achievement of C. S. Lewis*. Dr. Howard's bibliography includes a long list of journal titles which have appeared in such publications as *Christian Scholars Review, Catholic Digest, Christianity Today, Eternity, His, Christian Herald, New Oxford Review, Churchman, Modern Age, Reformed Journal, Episcopal Times*, and *The New York Times Book Review*.

The minute you start talking about Christianity and society in the same breath, you open Pandora's box, so to speak. All sorts of questions begin buzzing about your head.

How does Christianity see society, for example? On the surface of things, the answer might seem to be unimportant. What do we mean, how does Christianity see society? Society is simply there, and Christianity is there, and both have been muddling along for ages and ages, side by side. But here is the rub, of course. Is it side by side? Is Christianity to be thought of as existing next to something called society, the way Michigan lies next to Indiana, with both parties getting on with their business, offering more or less the same wares and amiably accepting

17

each other? After all, you can find a house in Michigan and a job, sometimes, and friends and diversions, just as you can in Indiana if you try hard enough. By the same token, depending on your tastes and your interests, you can find most of what you think you want in society: occupation, diversion, friends, fulfillment, hope, dignity, community, all these things that we all yearn for because we are human. On the other hand, if your tastes and interests are religious (goes this line of thought), then you can turn to Christianity, if you like, and occupy yourself with it. Or you can have both at once. I suspect this would be the formula for most people. We find that life itself takes up most of our time, what with getting and spending and family and friends and obligations of one sort or another. But if we think of ourselves as Christians, then we'll want to include going to church and saying our prayers in the agenda. It never seems to come down to any crux where we're obliged to pit our religion against our place in society. Ordinarily the matter doesn't seem to make too much difference.

Here are five houses along a neighborhood street, for example. All the families are more or less law-abiding and more or less amiable people, and all are busy with the things that make up life. If it happens that one of the families is Christian, and the rest of them non-religious, this will hardly show up except perhaps on Sunday morning when a car pulls out of one of the driveways and heads along the street. There they go to church.

It would seem, then, that we may think of Christianity as existing next to society in the sense that to all intents and purposes, we all have to live more or less identical lives as social creatures. And there are some of us who like a bit of religion thrown into the bargain, so we do our duties as Christians as well as citizens. But the two do not clash especially.

Now that is what is known as the superficial view. No reflective man can settle for it. Anyone who has given any thought to the matter knows that things are not that simple. The Bible, for instance, presents an odd view of society which deprives us of the luxury of supposing that Christianity and society never run afoul of each other. In the Old Testament, for example, the overriding assumption seems to be that the whole world is wicked and doomed and that God has picked Israel — tiny, unimportant Israel — to be a sort of showcase. In Israel you may see, if you'll bother to look, what human society ought to look like.

The Mosaic law sets things in order. To fear, love and worship the Most High is the first duty of man. And to live justly, and generously, and honestly with your neighbor is the next. Everything stands or falls with this scheme. Nothing else matters. The massed armies of Egypt, Assyria, Babylon, and Chaldaea are the merest pantomimes. The pyramids, the Hanging Gardens, the palaces, the monuments — these are the merest gauds. All the achievements of pagan civilization, seen from the Old Testament point of view, are of no interest or importance at all. The nations are as a drop in the bucket. Moab is my wash pot, says God.

This view of things seems to carry over into the New Testament. For one thing, the best we can get out of the Gospels concerning the relations between Christian and civilization is the injunction to pay our taxes, obey them that have the rule over us, do our work, and live honestly and justly. In all of His teaching, Christ mentions the most important man in the whole world (Caesar) only once. And then it is only with the assumption that some things, but not all things, are due to him. As for local potentates, the only reference Christ makes to Herod is to dismiss him as a fox. The only contact which the apostles had with civilization, and its authorities, consisted in trying to stay out of trouble, or jail.

Another point needs to be made here, namely that even when we carry the topic a step further than these merely political matters, and include the whole idea of "culture" in the word "society," we get nowhere with the Bible. There is not a syllable in either Testament by way of actually encouraging anyone to attach any importance to the things that constitute culture: music, art, poetry, drama, dance, architecture, philosophy, manners, class, fashion, cuisine, conversation. And yet in these activities we find the points at which human life begins to seem human, as opposed to bestial or barbarian. These are the important things. Politics, economics, diplomacy and war itself ought to exist in our minds as either threatening or protecting civilized, cultivated, human life.

But Christianity has very little, if anything, to say about culture. It is very distressing, especially for people who want to think of themselves as truly civilized, cultivated men and women. Indeed, it is sometimes the case that we feel it is important, if one is a Christian, to *be* cultured, to help counteract the notion that Christianity is for churls and fanatics and revivalists. We like to recall Chartres Cathedral and the Sistine Chapel, and King's College Chapel at Cambridge, not to mention Dante, and Sir Philip Sidney, and Cardinal Newman, when people begin speaking of Christianity in terms of the sawdust trail and stump preachers. Surely, we say, Christianity has been the great fountainhead of Western culture.

The minute we say this, however, we know that we have come upon a paradox, if not a dilemma, for we cannot speak of Western culture without invoking Athens as well as Jerusalem. And we cannot pretend that Athens and Jerusalem are cities at peace with each other. Athens and Jerusalem do not mean the same thing at all. If Athens is the noblest of earth's cities, it is still one of earth's cities, whereas Jerusalem, in Christian imagination, becomes synonymous with the City of God—the realm, in other words, which eventually overrides and swallows up the whole of human history and which remains unshaken when all other edifices have crumbled to dust like the statue of Ozymandias.

For some Christians, this presents no problem. For them Jerusalem stands starkly over against Athens. Christianity beckons us away from culture, away from civilization and society, to the Eternal Realm, they say. And there are God's plenty of Biblical texts to support this view: Here we have no continuing city; the world passeth away and the lust thereof, but he that doeth the will of God abideth forever; we seek for a city which hath foundations whose builder and maker is God. We, like the martyrs and heroes enumerated in the Book of Hebrews, confess that we are merely pilgrims and strangers here on this earth. St. Paul drives the point home remorselessly that nothing in heaven, earth, or hell matters except charity and sanctity.

And once again, the Gospels do not even nod in the direction of anything that we can remotely call culture. Everything seems designed to discourage us from any interest whatever, much less involvement, in culture and, *a fortiori*, in society.

Many Christian groups have seized on this line of thought and have bid adieu, so to speak, to society. All forms of puritanism to some extent represent the attempt to minimize earthly concerns and to live as simply as possible in the light of the heavenly calling laid upon us by Christianity. We ought not to permit the word puritanism to become a term of obloquy, by the way. It is an ancient and noble stream in Christianity, not confined to Protestantism. The Benedictine ideal may be said to be puritan in this sense of exhibiting austerity, and even exulting in it. As a way of life which bears witness to the amplitude of the divine life, the various Mennonite, Amish, Brethren, Moravian, and Quaker groups bear similar witness to a vision of things that sets very little store by history and its achievements. St. Francis of Assisi, in putting off his velvet and brocades and donning rough homespun, did not so much reject society and civilization as renounce them. This is a crucial distinction and may bring us towards the crux of our topic. To reject something is to disavow it as worthless or objectionable, or undesirable. But one may renounce something which is altogether good. Men do this when they go off to war and leave their wives and children behind. Or you do this when you get married: you renounce, in effect, your immediate loyalty to your parents and take up a different set of loyalties. Another claim has taken precedence over all that is lovely and rich and fruitful in your parents' house. There is one sense, of course, in which Christian imagination does reject "the world." It does so insofar as "the world" represents all that is egocentric, proud, avaricious, idolatrous, and lecherous. There can never be any alliance between Christianity and the fruits of those evil forces. The New Testament unabashedly uses the term "the world" to designate precisely anything that is anti-God. That is to be rejected. After all, it was this which crucified Christ, and Christians make the sign of the Cross on themselves, thus identifying themselves with Christ's dereliction at the hands of the world and embracing the Crucifixion as the glorious triumph of truth over the vanity and fraud of the world.

But, on the other hand, there is the Doctrine of Creation. The world—this planet, that is—and everything in it were made by God and he called it good. To be sure, there was no "society" or "civilization" in Eden. But society and civilization were there, as it were, in *germ*—in the intelligence and imagination which God bestowed on man and in his charge to man to multiply and to subdue the earth.

We ruined it all, before we ever got started, at the Fall; and from that day all of our efforts to build society have been tainted, botched and bedeviled with futility. Nevertheless, the Christian will see the whole effort of history itself—our remorseless struggle to subdue the wilderness and to build cities and to shape an existence for ourselves that is worthy of the name human and not merely bestial—a Christian will see all of this as some sort of response to the divine charge.

In this sense, then, Sodom itself becomes an image—an upside-down image, a botched image—of the City of God. It is ruinous, in that here we see men having become wholly consumed with self-indulgence, living with no reference to any fixed order presiding over their lives and determining their behavior. To that extent, Sodom would represent evil. But the very effort at life together at all—the trouble they went to to build this city—does it not bespeak something which touches on the very meaning of human life, and hence of divine life, since it is in the divine image that human life is made?

That something, which would be exhibited in any conceivable city, is community. We cannot live alone. We are social creatures. We need society. Our very attempts to design cities bear witness to this. From the Christian point of view, this is enormously significant. The fountainhead of human life is to be found in the mystery of the Holy Trinity where we find God existing, we are told, not in solitude, but in what can only be called fellowship, or society. The Father, the Son, and the Holy Ghost — not three Gods, but one. No language can unscramble the mystery here, of course: you can try to make your way through the Athanasian Creed if you think the matter is simple. But for our purposes here, it may suffice to say that at this fountainhead of human life, that is the divine life of the Holy Trinity, Christians perceive not solitude, but fellowship.

That fellowship, or what the 1950s called, in one of the most unfortunate words ever devised, "togetherness," becomes what we call society eventually. No one knows how things went in the early stages of history, of course. If we take the Book of Genesis as supplying us with an account of those early ages, we will find only the most sparse records. First there is Eden with all that the word conveys to us of harmony, tranquility, and plenitude, and in contrast to which we, like the Greeks and their Golden Age, find history to be a sad and frustrating affair. The very next place mentioned in Genesis is the land of Nod. Here is where Cain went, after he murdered his brother. What was Nod? Was anyone there? No one can say.

And then we find Cain building a city called Enoch, named after his son, and then there follows a jumbled record of marriages and murders: apparently society does not change very much over the millennia.

The point is that we build societies, and our task here is to inquire into just what view Christianity obliges us to take vis-à-vis these societies — or society shall we say.

As we have already observed, there is a paradox at the heart of the Christian understanding of society. On the one hand, we may perceive in the phenomenon of society itself at least two hints: first, here is humanity's obedience to the divine charge to be fruitful and to subdue the earth; second, here we announce ourselves as creatures who must have community. And to this extent, says Christianity, we bespeak, or evince, the image of God in us. We are social creatures. (Now someone will intervene here with beehives and anthills and ask whether bees and ants are also to be thought of as having been made in the image of God, if community is the great sign of that image, since they are certainly social creatures. A Christian would answer that *any* notion of community, on any level of life, will find its source eventually in the mystery of the Trinity, but that intelligent, voluntary, discriminating community is a special property of human community which bespeaks the image of God in ways not so clearly exhibited among the animals. And, of course, community is not the only quality in which we evince the Image of God: our reason, our will, our imagination, must all somehow bear on the matter.)

A Christian then will take the highest possible view of society. For him, society's credentials are far more august than any merely social contract. For a Christian, society's credentials lie ultimately in the being of God. So to this extent, Christianity invests the idea of society with more dignity than secularism does.

But then we come to the other pole of the paradox. Secularism has nothing *but* society, we might say, and hence, must invest the notion of society with ultimate significance, or at least with as much significance as you can get if you deny ultimates. Christianity, on the other hand, puts us in an ambiguous position towards society for two reasons. First, society is transitory, and a Christian is supposed to set his affections on things above, not on things on the earth. God alone is to be the object of a Christian's aspirations. A Christian is supposed to invest his ultimate interests and energy and attention, not in stocks and bonds, nor in career, nor in success nor fame nor even in the furtherance of art and culture. Nothing matters ultimately but charity, in the Christian view. Hence, if you can get a Christian to talk about society at all you will find that he is handling the topic with a certain demurral. He does not think that he is talking about matters of ultimate importance.

Second, society is corrupt. It is shot through with evil. A somewhat poetic way of putting this would be to say that no matter how hard we mortals try to build Jerusalem, we always end up building Babylon.

It is easy enough to see this in political schemes. Every single political scheme ever proposed has promised the "good life" for everybody. Hitler himself does not win over the masses by promising gas ovens and torture chambers. The vision of a clean, energetic, productive, blue-eyed, Aryan society in Germany was an appealing one. And national socialism was the agency to bring it to pass. But something went awry. It never delivered those goods.

Marx and Lenin promised freedom and happiness for all, but somehow seventy years later, those rewards still seem to elude the workers and peasants of Albania, North Korea, and even Russia itself. The French Revolution did not set out with misery and chaos for its agenda, but that is what they got before they were through, with most of them climbing the steps to the guillotine in the footsteps of Louis XVI and Marie Antoinette. So much for *liberté*, *égalité*, and *fraternité*. It doesn't matter much when your head is in the basket.

Our own political fathers wanted "to establish justice, provide for the common defense, promote the general welfare, and secure the blessings of liberty to themselves and their posterity." They did the best they could. But are we all happy? Who of us, if he had the powers of a tsar, would not immediately make gigantic changes in American society?

The joker in the social pack can never be named in political treatises. All of politics has to talk about society without talking about the biggest factor there is. The joker in the pack is sin. No party platform can admit this, of course. Nor can it admit that all of its best-laid plans will "gang agley" because all of the ward politicians and city bosses and party members are sinners. That doesn't look encouraging in political brochures, and it doesn't win votes. But it is the bald truth. You do not have to be a Christian to recognize that it is cupidity and cynicism and avarice that botch things up every time. Hence, you need not be a Christian in order to suspect that any accounting of history and society in its political aspects that omits any reference to cupidity, cynicism, and avarice is to a great extent whistling in the dark.

If this awareness of corruption is dismaying on the political front, it is even more so on the cultural front. Everyone knows that politics is grubby; but we all like to think of culture as a sort of treasure chest of "the finer things." Here are all of mankind's noblest achievements — what we mentioned in an earlier connection: music, sculpture, architecture, philosophy, drama, poetry, cuisine, conversation, manners, and so forth. And many noble minds have looked here for our salvation. We need only think of such men as Matthew Arnold in the nineteenth century, I. A. Richards, the twentieth-century English literary critic, F. R. Levis, another literary critic, the Bloomsbury group, and even Gertrude Stein's circle in Paris, to recognize that many of the most civilized and sophisticated imaginations of the nineteenth and twentieth centuries did, in fact, hope that society could be salvaged if we raised the level of everyone's *taste*. Finer discrimination is what is needed. Get the farmhands reading Petrarch. Organize evening classes in sculpture for the housemaids. Beat the bushes with Pico della Mirandola.

Alas, says the Christian. It won't do. Nothing could be more fatuous. Taste is very far from being the problem. People are churls, not because their sensibilities have not been finely enough tuned, but because churlishness, which is merely a gross form of egotism, has poisoned the wellsprings of the human heart. The name of the poison is sin.

There is something embarrassing about insisting on this notion of sin in the middle of a discussion about society and culture. It seems a bit flatfooted. It sounds too much like the stump preacher. But, of course, the stump preachers need not be wrong on every point, and on this one they are right. Insofar as they put society's problems down to sin, they have on their side the doctors of the church, the fathers of the church, the apostles, the prophets, and our Lord Himself. No matter how much we wish it were true, it is simply not the case that culture, in the sense of elevated sensibilities, has anything to do with goodness. If it did, then we might expect to discover that the Florence of the Medici, or the Urbino of the Montefeltros, or the Versailles of Louis XIV, or the great Whig houses in Regency London, to be fountainheads of sanctity and goodness. But, alas, those salons and soirees and levees seldom had sanctity for their real agenda. If some grizzled prophet like

Ezekiel or Habakkuk had suddenly popped into one of those drawing rooms, he would have cried out "Woe!" and "Whoredom!" The silvery laughter, the repartee, the badinage, the rhetoric, and the *sprezzatura* may have given a certain panache to the whole thing, but the gimlet eyes of the prophet would have bored straight through to the worms beneath the gilt.

Lest you think that this is turning into a diatribe, I will come to my point, which is this: there *is* no Christian view of man in society that omits the notion of sin. There is a name for the view that does — it is called Pelagianism — and Christianity very early condemned this as a heresy. We are not naturally good, says Christian orthodoxy, no matter how much we, along with the good monk Pelagius, might wish we were. We cannot pull ourselves up by our own bootstraps. We cannot save ourselves. Our highest and noblest achievements, alas, are shot through with failure and, worse, with egocentrism, which is in some sense the original sin.

I sometimes point my own students to a rather dismaying irony. It is the stark fact that the world of culture — "the arts," if you will — has never, alas, been the matrix for virtue. It is dismaying because all of us who have very fine and very noble minds might wish that we could establish some connection between the arts and something salvific for mankind. And it is ironic because I, of all people, ought not to be pointing this out, since I earn my board and keep by teaching subjects like drama and poetry. Belles-lettres. The arts. I *want* my students' imaginations to be blown awake by the thunder of Homer, Virgil, Dante, and Shakespeare. I want their vision to be stretched, to take in the whole firmament that arches like a titantic canopy of splendor over our experience — that firmament that holds constellations named Sophocles, Plato, Giotto, Mozart, Dostoevski. As a teacher, I would be guilty of treason if I withheld the achievements of these men from my students.

But — here is the irony — look at the world that surrounds the theatre. Test the fabric of the lives that pursue poetry or painting or music or dance as ends in themselves. What do we find? The data are not very encouraging. Perhaps we can dramatize the point this way: to whom shall we go when the foundations are shaken? Will we want to find the clever playwright who has cast mockery on middle-class foibles and celebrated adultery with lilting wit? Will we seek out the poet, lecherous as a sparrow, who reads his icon-smashing verse from 10,000 university podiums? Will we head for the brokers of taste—the painters and choreographers and sculptors who have presented us with violently accurate images of our alienation? Shall we go to the critics who instruct us as to what is chic this week? Or will we look for a Mother Teresa or a Simone Weil, or the plain, obscure householders and clerks, who by patient continuance in well-doing have learned something about the plain, coarse fabric of humdrum human life?

This is a caricature, of course. I do not wish to suggest that the poets are all lechers, or that the critics are all fatuous. I am drawing on popular stereotypes, I know. And I am not so naive as to suppose that the little householders are all gems of purest ray serene. But I think you follow my point. It is simply that it is impossible to establish any connection between fineness of *taste* and virtue. Or put it this way: even the poetry which celebrates virtue—and here we have Virgil and Shakespeare and even Chaucer at his bawdiest—even this poetry seems impotent when it comes to actually enabling us to *live* virtuously.

I am not exulting in the point. I teach Shakespeare, and I have never yet taught *Lear* or *Measure for Measure*, or any of the other plays, without finding myself agog at the sheer splendor of the moral vision at work there, and without hoping most earnestly that my students will catch a glance of that splendor— a glimpse that might, if only for a moment, pierce the thick and stupefying pall of sheer banality that has been cast over everything by rock culture. But I also have to admit that *King Lear* itself, perhaps the noblest of Shakespeare's plays and one of the most trenchant in its moral perspicacity, cannot be set beside the smallest of Saint John's epistles, say, or the most minor of the minor prophets.

Why is this? As a student of civilization and of humane letters, I wish I could pretend that there is an impenetrable conundrum here. I wish I had the luxury of loitering, bemused, in the precincts of this riddle which seems somehow to hint that these little epistolary scraps from a first-century religious zealot like Saint John stand on some higher absolute rung than *King Lear*. And, of course, in one sense the juxtaposition of the two is unfair. It is like comparing the proverbial apples and oranges. You can't choose between a letter and a play. But we are speaking here of a quality which is germane to both pieces of writing, namely, the quality, not only of nourishing moral vision, but of enabling us to live morally. The mere humanist would hope that *King Lear* would win the contest. The Christian humanist recognizes the irony, but finds himself obliged, on this point at least, to come down on the side of Saint John.

Why? The simplest answer—and it is the correct one theologically—is that in Saint John we find the Word of God and in Shakespeare, we find the word of man. There is no way around that for Christians who wish to locate themselves in the lineage of ancient orthodoxy. The Bible is *sui generis*. It alone is actually "quick and powerful and sharper than any two-edged sword, piercing to the dividing asunder of soul and spirit and of the joints and marrow, and is a discerner of the thoughts and intents of the heart," says Hebrews. The Bible alone ultimately is "profitable for doctrine, for reproof, for correction, for instruction in righteousness, that the man of God, the Christian, may be perfect, thoroughly furnished unto all good work."

These observations bring us to a point which has been much mulled over by Christian thinkers. In a sense it is the question with which we began. Our title is "Mere Christianity: A Focus on Man in Society." The whole question ranges along this frontier, as it were, where Christianity touches the notion of society. Does Christianity present us with an alternative society in the Church? Does Christianity abominate human society? Does Christianity beckon us away from human society and culture? Or does it nourish and enrich culture and bring human efforts and aspirations to their true fullness and liberty? Does it scorn human enterprises as feeble, vain, and transitory? Or does Christianity encourage and honor these human enterprises, whether they are political, social, or cultural, and see "common grace" flickering in them?

We will all be aware of the contrasting answers that have been given to these questions by Christians. Tertullian and all who follow in his train, including the great Saint Augustine himself, would stress the fallenness of human nature to the point of outright rejecting, or at least casting grave doubt on, the whole enterprise of human culture and society. Others of the Fathers, and the Renaissance Platonists who thought of themselves as being Christian, and the Christian humanists of the northern Renaissance, who certainly were Christian, such men as Erasmus, Colet, St. Thomas More, and more recent figures like Cardinal Newman and T. S. Eliot, would have urged that we cannot quite dismiss the human cultural enterprise so easily. Perhaps in doing so, we find ourselves rejecting some glimmers of the light that came into the world and lights every man. Even C. S. Lewis, who was very far from attaching the importance to culture that T. S. Eliot did, spoke of mythology, for example, as "gleams of celestial strength falling on a jungle of filth and imbecility."[1]

What we need to note here is that even granting the filth and imbecility—and who that has read his mythology will quarrel with this?—we may still see some gleams of celestial strength and beauty, at least if we share Lewis's view.

I cannot do better at this point, perhaps, than to refer you to some excerpts which I have taken from a number of Christian minds, all of which have addressed themselves to this question of the relationship between one's being Christian and one's finding oneself a member of human society. It is not a new question. All the comments below approach the question from the particular direction of education. Some of them ask what a man should read, for example. We may phrase the question this way: Is what the pagans have written about man in society

---

[1]C. S. Lewis, *Perelandra* (New York: Macmillan Publishing Co., Inc., 1944), p. 201.

worthy material for Christian imagination to feed itself on, or is it not?

Here is Saint Augustine. He felt that the point of education was "to learn the art of words, to acquire that eloquence that is essential to persuade men of your case, to unroll your opinions before them . . . to give pleasure through (the) argument." Augustine, to that extent, felt that his pagan education was valid. But then his great biographer, Peter Brown, puts it this way: "Augustine never faced the problem of replacing classical education throughout the Roman world. He merely wished to create for the devotees of true Wisdom an oasis of literary culture that was distinguished by being unself-conscious, unacademic, uncompetitive, and devoted to the understanding of the Bible alone . . ." But Augustine's own superbly unaffected "Christian" style was in reality a simplicity achieved on the other side of vast sophistication.[2]

Here is St. Thomas More ruminating about what a good society might look like, and talking about the citizens of his Utopia: "They define virtue as living according to nature. We have been ordained, they say, by God to this end. To follow nature is to conform to the dictates of reason in what we seek and avoid." Again both these words, nature and reason, have been spoiled in the modern age for us. Nature has come to mean "back to the earth" and reason has come to mean mere cerebration or intellect. To the Renaissance Christian humanist, however, reason meant the highest faculty has been given to us by God to judge, to discriminate between good and evil. And More says the first dictate of reason is "ardently to love and revere the Divine Majesty . . . secondly . . . to lead our lives as calmly and cheerfully as we can, and to help all others to attain this good."[3]

You will notice that every one of these men seems to have virtue at the center of his vision of what society should be nourishing.

---

[2]Peter Brown, *Augustine of Hippo: A Biography* (London: Faber & Faber, 1967), pp. 267, 268.

[3]St. Thomas More, *Utopia*, ed. and trans. H. V. S. Ogden (New York: Appleton-Century-Crofts, 1949), p. 48.

Here is Sir Thomas Eliot, sixteenth-century educationist, in his *The Book of the Governor*. He says that understanding "is the principal part of the soul, which is occupied about the beginning or original causes of things. Seneca saith, we instruct our children in liberal sciences, not because those sciences may give any virtue, but because they prepare the mind and make it apt to receive virtue."

Sir Philip Sidney, in his defense of poetry, says of poets, ". . . these indeed do merely make to imitate, and they imitate what God has made, both to delight and to teach, and delight to move men to take that goodness in hand which without delight they would fly as from a stranger, and teach to make them know that goodness whereunto they are moved." He goes on to say virtue is the most excellent resting place for all worldly learning to make its end of.

Milton says, "The end, then, of learning is to repair the ruins of our first parents by regaining to know God aright, and out of that knowledge, to love Him. . . . but, because our understanding cannot in this body found itself but on sensible things, nor arrive so clearly to the knowledge of God and things invisible, as by orderly conning over the visible and inferior creature, the same method is necessarily to be followed in all discreet teaching. . . ." By this time, years and good general precepts will have furnished them (that is, the young learners) more distinctly with that act of reason which in ethics is called Proairesis (the judgment of good and evil).

Here is C. S. Lewis on Cardinal Newman:

> Here at last I found an author who seemed to be aware of both sides of the question; for no one ever insisted so eloquently as Newman on the beauty of culture for its own sake, and no one ever so sternly resisted the temptation to confuse it with things spiritual. The cultivation of the intellect, according to him, is 'for this world'; between it and 'genuine religion' there is a 'radical difference'; it makes 'not the Christian . . . but the gentleman', and looks like virtue 'only at a distance'; he will not for an instant allow that it makes men better.[4]

---

[4]C. S. Lewis, *Christian Reflections* (Grand Rapids, Mich.: William B. Eerdmans Publishing Co., 1967), p. 18.

Lewis continues,

My general case (is) . . . that culture is a storehouse of the best (sub-Christian) values. These values are in themselves of the soul, not the spirit. But God created the soul. Its values may be expected therefore to contain some reflection . . . of the spiritual values. They will save no man. They resemble the regenerate life only as affection resembles charity, or honour resembles virtue, or the moon the sun. But though 'like is not the same', it is better than unlike. Imitation may pass into initiation. For some it is a good beginning. For others, it is not; culture is not everyone's road into Jerusalem, and for some it is a road out.

There is another way in which it may predispose to conversion. The difficulty of converting an uneducated man nowadays lies in his complacency. Popularized science, the conventions or 'unconventions' of his immediate circle, party programmes, etc., enclose the uneducated man in a tiny windowless universe which he mistakes for the only possible universe. There are no distant horizons, no mysteries. He thinks that everything has been settled. A cultured person, on the other hand, is almost compelled to be aware that reality is very odd, and that the ultimate truth, whatever it may be, *must* have the characteristics of strangeness — *must* be something that would be seen remote and fantastic to the uncultured. Thus, some obstacles to faith have been removed already.

On these grounds I conclude that culture has a distinct part to play in bringing certain souls to Christ. Not all souls — there is a shorter, and safer, way which has always been followed by thousands of simple affectional natures who begin, where we hope to end, with devotion to the Person of Christ.

Has (culture) any part to play in the life of the converted? I think so, and in two ways: (a) If all the cultural values on the way up to Christianity, if they were all dim antepasts ectypes of the truth, we can recognize them as such still. And since we must rest and play, where can we do so better than here — in the suburbs of Jerusalem? It is lawful to rest our eyes in moonlight — especially now that we know where it comes from, that it is only sunlight at second hand; (b) Whether the purely contemplative life is, or is not, desirable for any, it is certainly not the vocation of all. Most men must glorify God by doing to His glory something which is not *per se* an act of glorifying but which becomes so by being offered. If, as I now hope, cultural activities are innocent and even useful, then they also (like the sweeping of the room in Herbert's poem) can be done to the Lord. The work of a charwoman and the work of a poet become spiritual in the same way and on the same condition. . . . Let us stop giving ourselves airs.[5]

I am aware that I have stressed the "cultural" aspect of the topic before us today. Christianity may focus on man in society at various points. My assumption has been that in the achievements which are ordinarily to be found under the general heading of culture, we may find suggestions as to what man has thought society was all about.

If we may take the remarks which I have just read for you from Augustine and Milton and Newman and others as indicating some of the lines along which Christian thought has run when it has pondered the question of Christianity's relation to human culture, then we may say that Christian imagination does find a certain tension. None of the Christian humanists are prepared to jettison human culture summarily. But neither would any of them see human culture, even at its best, as necessarily contributing to virtue. And being Christian, they are all obliged to settle for virtue as the only really crucial thing to be sought by mankind. Taste, urbanity, reticence, breadth of sympathy, fineness of sensibility, gravity of judgment, prudence, austerity—these are all good things, and may be begotten and nourished at the pagan spring, so to speak. But as for deliverance from the ambiguities that bedevil man in society, and from the dilemma with which man in society is beleaguered, that will only truly be found, if we may agree with Augustine and St. Thomas More and Newman, in the Word of God. The attempt to skirt this will always land us back in paganism, or in heresy, or in some other departure from mere Christianity.

---

[5]*Ibid.*, pp. 23, 24.

God and Man's Science: A View of Creation

Stanley L. Jaki

Dr. Stanley L. Jaki was born in Hungary where he entered the Benedictine Order in 1942. After completing his undergraduate training in philosophy, theology, and mathematics, he was ordained in 1948. He received his S.T.D. (doctor of sacred theology) from the Rome Instituto Pontificio di S. Anselmo, and his Ph.D. in physics from Fordham where he studied under Nobel Laureate Victor F. Hess, discoverer of cosmic rays. Jaki has done post-doctoral research in the history and philosophy of science at Princeton, Stanford, and the University of California, Berkeley. He was only the sixth American invited by the University of Edinburgh to deliver the Gifford Lectures. Dr. Jaki's lectures were published under the title *The Road of Science and Ways of God*. Jaki's articles have appeared in journals such as the *American Journal of Physics, ZYGON*, and *Scientia*. His latest book is a critical translation of Kant's *Universal Natural History and Theory of the Heavens*. Dr. Jaki is currently Distinguished University Professor, Seton Hall University.

The organizers of this week's special program have invited me to speak on "God and Man's Science: A View of Creation." For their suggesting the title, I am most grateful. They spared me the irksome task of having to make a choice. A gain is, however, always a loss. The title chosen stands for a vast topic which puts one at a loss about the always difficult problem of where to begin. Logic demands that the subtitle, "a view of creation," should not be the starting point. Logic may then suggest that we start with the main title, which begins with God.

Being the ultimate, God is certainly the first both logically and ontologically. However, our knowledge of God is not direct but indirect, that is, inferential. Our direct knowledge is about things and ourselves, which are the grounds of our inferential

35

knowledge about God. There is also to be kept in mind a lesson of modern Western philosophy. Some rationalists, such as Descartes and Spinoza, and some idealists, especially the Hegelians, were wont to begin with God. They invariably lost out on things and ended with themselves, the worst possible outcome.

We are then left with "man's science" as a starting point. The expression "man's science" is not, however, as simple a proposition as it may appear. It may mean, for instance, science about man, a terribly vast subject including anthropology, psychology, and medicine, none of which is my specialty. "Man's science" would much more be related to my own studies if the emphasis were to be put on science as such. In that case, one could deal with the philosophy and history of science. Part of that history is very human. There are indeed very good reasons for uttering the phrase "man's science" in a mournful tone. Some sad aspects of science have been very much in the news and therefore could serve as a starting point.

In some very sad sense, which is very human indeed, science is a very human enterprise. Among other things, science is mercilessly competitive. Science does have its tough entrepreneurs no less than does any branch of business. Stories, such as the story of the double helix, have amply revealed the fierce pursuit of prizes which go only to the very first and never to the best second, let alone to the second best. Enough is also reported through newspapers about the keen competition for research grants, for the funding of new equipment, for new laboratories and institutions—a competition which at times mobilizes the public opinion of entire states and even wider regions. Teams of anthropologists stake out claims for elusive distant valleys with no less rush and jealousy than was the case a hundred years ago with homesteaders and somewhat earlier with gold diggers in California.

There are also some cases, not too many though increasing in number, which show scientists cheating with their data. The pressure to come up with novel results, the pressure of having another paper published, is too great; to yield to that pressure, the pressure of opportunity, is all too human. Some prominent medical schools and research institutes indeed suffered very bad publicity in recent years because they failed to prevent such misdeeds, or to detect them soon enough. Science can indeed become very much man's science in a very sad sense.

There is also the ever-present human fallacy of wishful thinking: namely, the desire to see something where there is nothing. The case of those who claim to have seen balls moved by their mere mental concentration on them reveals plenty of the humanness of science in that very sad sense. Other, less known examples are the alleged discovery, early this century, of N-rays, and the claim made about ten years ago of experimental evidence of a very slight difference between the negative and positive electric charge. That some scientists take upon themselves the role of universal sages, pontificating on any and all problems and issues, is more evidence of science being very much man's science—that is, a very human affair.

Another aspect of the humanness of science is more tragic. Three hundred years ago, at the time of Newton, when science appeared robustly on the scene, it was greeted by many as the means whereby paradise may be created on earth. In 1664 Henry Power, a junior member of the Royal Society, greeted science as the tool for which "there is no Truth so abstruse, nor so far elevated out of our reach, but man's wit may raise Engines to Scale and Conquer it." A hundred years later Joseph Priestley, an English scientist, fled to the United States in a similar state of mind. He felt that in the virgin fields of this newly born country there would be a better chance of implementing the new and final age of mankind, an age "glorious and paradisiacal beyond what our imagination can now conceive."

These United States of ours have indeed proved a fertile ground for that optimism which saw in science only the harbinger of happiness and prosperity. For the past hundred years, the notion of a rather naive progress could thrive in our midst in coexistence with a doctrine, Darwinism, which in fact offered progress (or mere survival) for only a relatively few and meekly condoned the perishing of the great majority in each class, group, or species, if you wish. Social Darwinism saw its heyday in our country not too long ago. In fact, it still has a few rearguard apostles who are not taken aback even by the obvious, such as the late J. Bronowski. He could go to such extremes as to exculpate science of any and all responsibility concerning Hiroshima and Nagasaki.

As is well known, because of science, man's science, man can trigger a chain reaction of genetic mutation ruining the entire human race. Because of science, man's science, man can ruin his entire environment and blow himself into outer space on the wings of mushrooming nuclear blasts. The mind-boggling extent to which man has turned the finest inventions of science to destructive purposes cannot be given a better summary than the one given by Captain Ahab of *Moby Dick* about his own tragic course: "All my means are sane, my motives and objects are mad."

The end, the scientifically engineered end, may of course come so very unobtrusively as to be seen as by default. No properly organized, internationally sponsored studies are in progress, for instance, about the ultimate impact of rocket exhaust deposited in the upper atmosphere of a height three times the one at which most commercial airliners now fly. That may ultimately result in a layer of carbon dioxide of such concentration as to turn the entire earth into a greenhouse in which the rise of temperature can no longer be reversed.

This is wise to recall when our attention is occasionally drawn from the thousands of space satellites serving military purposes to satellites of purely scientific aim. One of these carrying a telescope made headlines a month or so ago after registering radiation around Vega (26 million light years away), the source of which may be a ring of small particles. The spotting of such a radiation is a most extraordinary achievement. It could, however, be expected that around a fairly young star like Vega there would be a ring or belt of small particles, not much different from a thick gas. Unfortunately, it is also to be expected that such a ring would be readily taken for a proof of a planetary system in embryo, eventually able to carry life, intelligent life included.

The proof in question is a perfect example of another aspect of science which shows how human an enterprise science is, how much science is man's science. While the proof has been presented in countless headlines and reports as wholly reliable, it is in fact as full of holes as is a sieve or a colander. Around the turn of the century it was already demonstrated that a ring of particles can never gather into a single large body or planet. The demonstration was duly printed in a leading scientific journal, reported in other journals and books by prominent scientists, and mentioned in widely read books. Its validity has never been questioned. I told the whole story half a dozen years ago in one of my books. Since that book was published by such an eminent and leading scientific publishing house as John Wiley in New York, it had to be easily within the reach of anyone interested in factual evidence, an interest which is the presumed hallmark of scientific thinking. Why is it then that such an evidence fails to be translated into broad awareness? Why is it that in science, as in all other fields of human inquiry and enterprise, there is at work a very selective perception, very much akin to the so-called phenomenon of selective indignation?

The reason is connected with the role which science has come to play in shaping the intellectual atmosphere of our modern, Western intellectual world. That atmosphere is largely the making of the leaders of two generations, straddling the French Revolution. The leaders of the first, or earlier generation, were essentially though not entirely, dismantlers. Their immediate aim was to dislocate and annihilate the *ancien régime* and whatever was connected with it socially, politically, ideologically, and economically. Such people like Diderot and Condorcet knew, however, that a purely negative strategy never works. Something positive has to be dangled before the eyes of the so-called educated class, which is always the naive and indispensable tool of revolutionaries for whom the cause of the proletariat is all too often but a convenient cover-up. A central part of that positive program was science, which for the second generation was led by Comte and others and which became the principal preoccupation to exploit. It is certainly ironical, though not at all unexpected, that not much science was to be contained in that program in spite of its label, positivism. About science Diderot and Condorcet were most eager to claim not only that it would usher in a paradise on earth, but also that its rise implied a radical opposition to tradition, that is, to Christianity. A principal claim of those two was in fact that science, born in an anti-Christian, purely rationalist spirit, can fulfill its promises only if Christianity as a social matrix and presence is wholly discredited and discarded. This claim was immensely successful. It has produced an intellectual climate which has for the past 150 years found an expression in a few bestsellers. They all have been devoted to the contention that science and religion (Christian religion, of course) are utterly irreconcilable.

Such was indeed the gist of the claim of Diderot and especially of Condorcet about the origin and rise of science. Is it indeed true that science owes its origin to men that have turned their back to Christianity? Quite the contrary is the truth. The question of any historical origin is, of course, always a bit nebulous. Scholars will forever dispute the exact beginning of the Middle Ages, of the Renaissance, of Classicism, and of Romanticism, or for that matter as to who was the first modern thinker. There is always a hazy margin when it comes to the exact determining of any of the isms forming the principal chapters of Western intellectual history, or of any history for that matter. No one would, however, say that just because the exact beginning of those *"isms"* is difficult to determine, there was no true beginning for the Middle Ages, for the Renaissance, for Classicism and Romanticism. In fact, if any of these epochs is viewed against its immediate predecessor or its background, its reality strikes one with overwhelming force, and its origin will be easier to pinpoint.

Much the same applies to the question of the origin of science. The gift to its solution can easily emerge if seen against the background of great cultures that had no science. Among such great cultures were ancient China, ancient India, Egypt, Babylon and Greece. The case of the Chinese is particularly instructive because of a statement made by Francis Bacon in the early seventeenth century. According to Francis Bacon, science arose at that time because of three European inventions: gunpowder, the compass, and printing. That Francis Bacon did not speak of the old and Chinese origin of at least two of those inventions, the gunpowder and the compass, is a secondary matter. The principal point is that we had ascribed the origin of science to mechanical inventions. Now if Bacon had been right, one would expect the Chinese of old to have developed science. They did not. Had they done so, we would be today, I am afraid, part of a huge, worldwide Chinese empire. Please also recall that at the time of Vasco da Gama the Chinese navy was as good if not better than the Portuguese navy. The Chinese could have easily sailed along the Aleutians or across Midway and the Hawaiian islands and colonized the California coastline. They did not, luckily for us.

Since the Chinese of old served evidence of a great deal of inventiveness in mechanical skills, it is reasonable to assume that what they lacked was something of an intellectual insight for formulating and developing science. This assumption becomes well-nigh irresistible when we look at what happened in classical Greece. They failed to develop science, by which I mean an intellectual enterprise in which one discovery generates another discovery and does so at an increasingly accelerated rate. Not that they lacked scientific genius productive in intellectual insights — it is enough to think of Euclid's geometry or of Aristarchus's method of determining the size of the earth, moon and sun and their relative and absolute distances. Yet, the Greeks of old failed to make any breakthrough in the science of motion or dynamics which is the basis of all physics and which in turn is the basis of all modern exact science.

In speaking of the science of motion, Newton's name naturally comes to mind. Physics is Newtonian physics and even Einstein's physics would be inconceivable without Newton's *Principia*. That book begins with the three laws of motion: the basis of the whole science of mechanics, including rocket propulsion and space travel. Newton, of course, did not care to tell his readers how he arrived at those laws. He did not care because he was a very proud man unwilling to give credit to others, as was all too often the case with other seventeenth-century scientists and authors. Galileo and Descartes are two chief examples of this intellectual stinginess. Had Newton cared to say something about the origin of those three laws, and had he been utterly candid, he might have proceeded something like this: The credit for the third law (force equals mass times acceleration) belongs to me though not in the sense that I had formulated the notion of uniform acceleration. Credit for the latter should go to Galileo. As to the second and first laws, Newton should have made a special effort to be candid. The reason for this was that both those laws could be found in the books of Descartes, of whose reputation Newton was terribly jealous. He did not want anyone to ever learn that he owed anything to Descartes. In his later years, Newton in fact spent much previous time on erasing from his manuscripts and notebooks the name of Descartes, lest posterity may learn the truth.

Had Newton acknowledged Galileo and Descartes, he would have not stated thereby the true origin of the first law and of the law of acceleration of which the free fall of a body is a classic case and primary example. Descartes was not the inventor of the all-important first law, nor was Galileo the inventor of the no-less-important law of acceleration. They could find them (and indeed found them) in several books printed in the 1570s and 1580s, whose authors took them from an earlier tradition, antedating the invention of printing. That tradition can be traced to the fourteenth-century Sorbonne, especially to the lectures of John Buridan and his greatest disciple, Nicole Oreselm, who died as Bishop of Lisieux in 1378.

Lecturing in the fourteenth-century medieval universities consisted of reading the books of a prominent ancient author, very often Aristotle, and commenting on the text. This had by then been an old tradition going back to Hellenistic times and in particular to Muslim schools. One of Aristotle's scientific books which was most often commented upon was his cosmology, called *On the Heavens*. There Aristotle most explicitly states that the world is eternal and that its motion, and in particular the daily circular motion of the sphere of stars, is also eternal because the world is and must be uncreated, that is, without a beginning. Whatever else the Prime Mover of Aristotle was, he was not a Creator. Aristotle had only scorn for the idea of creation out of nothing. For Aristotle, the world, the universe, the cosmos, was the ultimate entity, likely identical in its better or celestial parts with the Prime Mover himself. The cosmos, according to Aristotle, had necessarily to be what it is — in no way could the Prime Mover fashion, let alone create, a different universe.

Newton's first law was formulated by medieval schoolmen in reaction against such and similar statements of Aristotle and of other pagan classical scholars who held those statements to be absolute dogmas. The eternity and uncreatedness of the universe was indeed the chief dogma of all pagan religions, old and new, crude and refined. The medieval reaction to that dogma was, as one could expect it, made in terms of the first dogma of Christian Creed, the dogma of creation of all time, that is, in the beginning. How productive and fruitful that reaction was for science can be seen in John Buridan's commentaries on Aristotle's *On the Heavens*. After rejecting Aristotle's doctrine on the eternity of motion, Buridan wrote: "In the beginning when God made the heaven and the earth, He imparted a certain amount of impetus (motion) to the stars which impetus they still keep because they move in a space where there is no friction." This statement, which is essentially equivalent to Newton's first law, reappeared in many medieval lecture notes and appeared in print many times before Descartes came to the scene.

Since there is no time to discuss the pre-Galilean history of acceleration, let us turn to Newtonian science, of which the law of acceleration is a pivotal proposition in the form of the well-known force law. That law of motion and the first two do not yet make science. Newton's greatness lies, first, in his claim that his laws of motion are universally valid and second, that he had shown something of that universality. I mean his proof that the motion of the moon is governed by the same acceleration as is the fall of an apple or stone to earth. This coupling of the earth and of the moon was a bold step into the universe of things. It revealed in a single stroke the very essence of science, which is the universal applicability of its laws. This is what is meant by the phrase that all science is cosmology, that is, all science is about the cosmos or the universe. This is why every really fundamental law of physics reveals something all-encompassing about the universe; this is why almost all readily great physicists write pages, at times entire chapters, and on rare occasions, entire books which are equivalent to a cosmology either in outline or fully developed.

There are several pages in Newton's writings which are equivalent to a cosmology. A few of those pages appeared in Newton's time, another few about thirty years after his death, and still another few very important and revealing pages only about twenty or so years ago. All those pages show two things: First, Newton's preference was for a universe which was finite and spherical, floating in an infinite space filled with the ether which he did not hold to be matter in the ordinary sense. That such was Newton's preference can easily be gathered from the *Spectator*, a magazine whose editor, Addison, was a good acquaintance of Newton. In the July 9, 1714 issue of the *Spectator*, Addison in fact wrote that according to Newton and reason, the world is finite in an infinite space. This phrase was then taken over by Voltaire in his book on Newton's physics, a book which saw over 25 editions prior to the nineteenth century.

The other thing to remark about Newton's cosmology is that he bungled about the scientific merit of a truly infinite material universe in which stars could be found to infinity in any direction. I said bungled because he was told about a proof which convincingly showed that such a universe entailed a scientific contradiction. Newton rejected the proof perhaps because it was formulated not by a scientist, but by a classical scholar, Richard Bentley, who was also Master of Trinity College, Newton's own college, and a rather overbearing clergyman to boot. However that may be, the proof of Bentley was given an exact formulation almost 200 years later. According to that formulation, the gravitational potential in an infinite universe of homogeneously distributed stars is infinite at any point. Such a universe cannot exist physically.

The origin and whole history of the so-called Newtonian universe shows something of man's science in two different senses. One is the greatness of man's mind as evidenced by his science. Newton's third law, which is the basis of his law of gravitation, proved exceedingly powerful. It enabled subsequent scientists, such as Euler, Herschel, and Laplace, to explain most peculiar features of the motion of planets and of distant double stars. In other words, the science of Newtonian gravitation was truly a science because it allowed man to reach far into the cosmos. But Newtonian gravitation could not give a scientific account of the universe, inasmuch as the universe was taken for a so-called infinite Newtonian universe. That such a universe was not rejected categorically by Newton and that in the nineteenth century it became generally believed in is the other sense of Newtonian science being but man's science. For all its greatness, the scientific mind is not infallible. In its reasonings it came to be the victim of foibles, of biases, of prejudices and even of sheer blindness to the obvious.

For us, late twentieth-century men, Newtonian science is a thing of the past. Everybody knows that Newton has been superseded by Einstein, but very people know the true reason for this. The usual reason given is that Einstein showed everything to be relative. Nothing could be farther from the truth. Einstein's theory of General Relativity is the most absolutist theory ever proposed in the history of science. In fact, the entire success of Einstein's theory is that it is absolutist. According to it, the value of the speed of light is independent of any reference systems and therefore has a value which is absolutely valid. According to the same theory, all inertial and accelerated reference systems are absolutely equivalent. Being a great scientist, Einstein also worked out a cosmology. Since he knew that the three-dimensional Newtonian universe was an impossibility, he had to turn to a four-dimensional framework. There are several forms of a four-dimensional space-time manifold, such as a cylindrical space or hyperbolical space, which are compatible with an infinite mass. But these solutions seemed to Einstein to be too peculiar, and therefore to contradict the principle of simplicity. So he took a four-dimensional manifold in which the motion of material particles can only be circular. As a consequence of this he had to regard the finite and material universe as spherical. Within a year or so, in 1917, another scientist, Willem de Sitter, found that Einstein's spherical universe was unstable. At the slightest disturbance in it, that is, at the slightest motion of any of its parts, be they galaxies, stars or atoms, such a universe had to expand. Einstein was not at all happy with this finding, but this is another story.

We are now at the theoretical origin of what is today called the expansion of the universe. In the 1920s, the rate of expansion was predicted and soon verified by the recessional red shift observed in the spectrum of most galaxies. If, however, the universe is expanding, there has to be a time in the past when it was very small, perhaps as small as an atom.

To speak of the early universe as an atom was very appropriate in the atomic age. The discovery of atoms and of the atomic structure of all the chemical elements led to speculations about the genesis of those elements. Around 1950 a rather promising theory was formulated about the condition in which electrons and protons could unite into hydrogen, hydrogen into helium, helium into lithium, and then into the heavier elements. The gist of that theory was a hypothetical early state of the universe in which the universe consisted only of photons, electrons, protons, and neutrons. Such a universe was in a rapid expansion and dropped through a very specific temperature and pressure range. Most importantly, such a universe had to leave behind a very specific radiation, which was in fact detected in 1963.

Since then, many other advances have been made in scientific cosmology, the hottest field of research in science today. All these findings are expressive of two all-important facts. The first is that man's science is so marvelously powerful a thing as to give man the ability to have a real, that is, scientifically reliable grasp of the universe. The second is that the view given by science about the universe is a very special view. In that view, the universe appears to be a most peculiar, most specific entity. Being very specific, the universe is not different from any other thing. All things are terribly specific. Precisely because they are very specific, they reveal, indeed they suggest with a brute force, that they could be different from what they are. In other words, specificity always reveals the non-necessary character of a thing or anything. This is precisely what is revealed by modern science about the universe as a most specific entity. Now if the universe is not necessary, that is, not necessarily what it is, then it is contingent. If, however, it is contingent, its actual shape and its very existence are dependent on a choice which transcends the entire universe. Such a choice or power can only be the creative omnipotence of God. Such is the chain of events of reasonings which show that man's science is not only a view of the universe but also a view of creation and that ultimately we have to begin with God. Both history and logic show that God, the Christian God, is needed in order to let man have science, and if that science is truly a science or cosmology, man's view of the universe becomes a view of creation.

Such an outcome, as one would expect, is most repulsive to secular humanists. They are as numerous among scientists in general and cosmologists in particular as they are in any other professional group. In fact, they should seem all the more numerous because secular publishers (including university presses) are much more willing to publish their writings than writings done in the vein, for instance, of this lecture. The pattern is "secular" in the meaning of long-standing. Thirty years ago all the publicity, including the very important marketing of inexpensive paperbacks, was given to the proponents of the so-called steady-state universe. The chief aim of that theory was to take out of cosmology the metaphysical sting which was brought into it by the expanding universe. Since that expansion forcefully showed the time-conditioned contingent character of the universe, the steady-state-universe theorists, some of them professed atheists, postulated that the average density of matter in the universe, which decreases by the expansion, is compensated by the appearance, out-of-nothing and without a Creator, of new hydrogen atoms in the space left empty by the receding galaxies. Of course, they did their best to give a scientific rationale to that antimetaphysical, antirational, and antiscientific extravaganza. They pointed at a discrepancy, now completely resolved, of the age of stars and the age of the universe. The very fact that within a few years the discrepancy was resolved shows how minor a problem it really was and how extravagant it was to propose for its solution a most extraordinary process, namely, the steady creation, without a creator, of hydrogen atoms out of nothing. The solution, extravagant even from the purely philosophical viewpoint, was defective also from the strictly scientific viewpoint for two reasons. First, no such radiation was detected. Most importantly, it did not follow at all scientifically that even if there had been observed an extra amount of 21 cm radiation characteristic of an H atom, nothing should be assigned as the immediate antecedent of that radiation. The nothing is never an object of scientific, that is, partly empirical, inference. Yet for all such outstanding defects in the steady-state theory, it had been touted for two decades as one of the three most respectable cosmologies.

The two other models were the model of a single-expansion and the oscillating model. The latter has been turned into another smoke screen against the view of the universe as God's creation. Like the steady-state theory, the oscillating model, too, had very serious scientific problems. But in the so-called higher popularizations of that model, those problems have been systematically ignored for obviously secularist or materialist reasons. In the oscillating universe, one world-age, or expansion-contraction cycle, would be followed by another in endless sequence. Once that sequence is taken to be really endless, then it is readily taken for a proof of the eternity of the world, which is the very opposite to the Christian dogma of creation. According to that dogma, the world was created in time; that is, the past time-span of the existence of the world is strictly finite. There is another conflict between the Christian notion of a created universe and the oscillating model. A created universe embodies purpose, whereas a universe oscillating forever stands for the very opposite. It stands in fact for an eternal treadmill in which worlds and civilizations would follow one another and repeating one another in an endless sequence.

Time does not allow but a mere mention of other cosmological models serving a distinctly secularist, agnostic, and materialistic purpose. One of them is called the multiworld model in which there are as many universes as there are observers. How one observer can communicate with another observer, that is, get out of his own world into another world, is not explained in that theory. Another such model is the model of an accidental universe. Its chief promoter, W. P. Davies, a British scientist, has just come out, not surprisingly, with a book in which science is pitted against Christian religion. That nothing happens by accident is, of course, a chief tenet of Christian religion, according to which not even a sparrow falls to the ground, or a hair is bent on our head, without our Heavenly Father willing it. That nothing happens by accident—that is, by sheer chance, that is, really without a cause—is also a chief tenet of science about the material universe. For if anything were truly accidental, there could be no consistency, and without consistency there could be no laws, not even statistical laws, because even they imply one or two parameters which imply consistency. In fact, the best and latest scientific discoveries or laws about the universe show us a universe which is the embodiment of the highest degree of consistency, both in space and in time. Indeed, everything is so consistently interconnected in the universe as modern science reveals it to us that an account of the extreme specificity of the primeval condition of the universe permits the inference that only in such a universe could arise man, who is even more specific or peculiar than the universe itself. While the universe does not know itself, man knows both himself and the universe. More importantly, he can see beyond both the first and the ultimate which is God. All this and much more should come to mind in speaking of God and man's science or a view of creation.

Augustine's Political Philosophy?

Gerhart Niemeyer

Dr. Gerhart Niemeyer studied at the Universities of Cambridge, Munich, and Kiel prior to becoming a naturalized American citizen in 1943 while serving as assistant professor, Princeton University. Dr. Niemeyer later served as head of the history division at Oglethorpe, a foreign affairs officer for the U.S. State Department, and a research analyst for the Council on Foreign Affairs. He is currently Professor Emeritus at Notre Dame, where he served as professor from 1955 to 1976. He has been a visiting professor at Hillsdale College, Yale, Columbia, and Vanderbilt. In 1962, Dr. Niemeyer was awarded a Fulbright professorship at the University of Munich. An ordained Episcopalian priest, Dr. Niemeyer has written widely in the fields of theology and ideology. Among his major titles are *Law Without Force, Facts on Communism*, Volume I, *The Communist Ideology*, and *Between Nothingness and Paradise*.

Responsible philosophical critique of philosophy is rare, but the few who achieve it today speak with a new tone of authority. Their argument has new weight because the horizon has widened. On the one hand, many excellent books have given us new insight into the order of the myth, "before philosophy." On the other hand, equally impressive research has been done into the antiphilosophical and antitheistic idea structures known as "ideologies," which are at the root of the deep and widespread disorientation of our time. Between these two horizon-points, philosophy has come into view as a whole, so to speak. We see it as the historical event of the discovery of rational human consciousness, set off against the myth as well as against the annihilating tidal wave of ideologies. At the same time, we now "see" it in terms of its own development, with landmarks that can be

assumed as familiar in educated discussion. Landmark thinkers, *e.g.*, Descartes and Hegel, serve the need for an historical
overview.

I submit that another such thinker is Augustine of Hippo,
ranking foremost in the enterprise of philosophizing in the
mode of antiquity but with the insights of Christian faith.
Unlike other landmark thinkers, Augustine is known only
superficially, and even then only through the glasses of errone-
ous clichés. Furthermore, the element of Christian doctrine in
his work tends to block an understanding of Augustine for
many modern non-Christian thinkers, although first-rate
scholars have never been deterred by the absence of their personal identification with the object of their study.

Looking at Augustine as a philosopher of politics brings up
another difficulty. Augustine is mostly known as the originator
of philosophy of history. Some have felt that this is the appearance of Augustine when seen from the standpoint of modern
times, so that one may well ask whether, in his own time,
Augustine really created a philosophy of history.[1] May one not
equally ask, then, "Was Augustine a philosopher of politics?"
There are no later political theorists who designate themselves
"Augustinians." For that matter, though, there are also no philosophers of history who claim to be Augustinians, and yet few
people doubt that history, as "the symbolic form of our consciousness," goes back to Augustine. Augustine, then, really did
not teach political theory to others.

Still, let us place him in the broad historical context of philosophy from Athens's fifth century B.C. on. For almost 150
years, the Greeks were astonishingly productive in that field of
politics. After the brief and labile self-expression of that school
of the Greek Enlightenment, the Sophists, there came the
deeply serious and mystical response of Plato's *Republic*, and
Aristotle's great attempt to build a political science in the
framework of fundamental ethics. But then nothing similar

---

[1]Ernest L. Rortin, "Augustine's City of God and the Modern Historical
Consciousness," *Review of Politics* 41/3 (July 1979).

happened for hundreds of years. The two Greek productions, one frivolous and the other, attentive and responsive, were not continued and developed. Cicero's works, *The Republic* and *The Laws*, brought nothing new. From Cicero to Augustine, fully 450 years, most philosophers did not touch politics at all. In the fifth century A.D., however, Augustine did give a great deal of attention to politics, and not as an epigone, but in the context of a most innovative ontology, cosmology, anthropology, and ethics. Even this brief glance would tell us that, in view of earlier Church Fathers who dismissed public order from the perimeter of Christian concerns, Christianity, without Augustine, might not have developed a civilization of its own, or else might have developed an apolitical culture resembling, for instance, Buddhism. The rank of a landmark philosopher, then, cannot be denied Augustine even in the field of politics.

I

For reasons of comparison let us draw up, in schematic form, the work of Aristotle and Plato in political science.

Plato: An anthropology centering on an analysis of the three parts of the soul, and an hermeneutics of the basic experiences of *erōs*, *thanatos*, and *daimōn*; a concept of justice derived from the hierarchical order of the three parts of the soul; a verbal model of "the idea" of the state in terms of institutional arrangements that would, if realizable, put an end to "the troubles of the world"; an exploration of the four cardinal virtues; a scheme of public education; a concept of man's experience of, and capacity for, participation in the divine source of order, the *nous*; the concept of political rule by the philosopher; a description of the psychological, cultural, and political dynamics of successively deteriorating stages of perverted order, with tyranny as the nadir.

Aristotle: An anthropology based on the concept of four ranks of being, and an analysis of the two parts of the human soul; the concept of happiness as the highest good; a descriptive and ana-

lytical list of virtues, with justice as that virtue which comprises
all the virtues; the concept of the *spoudaios*, the self-ruling
mature man who loves the *nous* within him; a genetic theory of
the state; an evaluative classification of forms of the state; a
sociology of various types of perverted society; an analysis of
political crisis; a concept of "the best state."

One should add that both Plato and Aristotle concerned themselves with the state because they were deeply concerned for the
soteria tou einai, the preservation of being against external
adversities and internal disorder. Plato saw the state required by
the disease, "the fever," of the "luxurious," *i.e.*, civilized state.
Aristotle considered the state a setting required by nature for
the secure attainment of a "happy" life in the midst of family,
friends, and fellow citizens, which life could be attained only by
the *spoudaios*, the man capable of ruling others because he
already ruled as king over himself. Both Plato and Aristotle had
the most serious doubts about the realizability of their models
of salvific political order: Plato said that "the idea" of the state
was not a community that could ever be found on earth; Aristotle did not believe that one could find any city with even one or
two *spoudaioi*. Still, both saw human life constantly threatened
by decline or destruction. The philosopher's task was to identify
the cause of this besetting insecurity of being in order to arrange
for some means of preventing this. Categorically, the counter-
action was called *soteria*, "deliverance, safety." Augustine's
Latin equivalent was *salus*, "health, soundness." Certainly
Augustine shared Plato's and Aristotle's concern for deliverance from life-destroying adversities. To what extent did this
concern motivate his philosophizing on political order?

II

That seems to be the fundamental question to ask in any comparison between Greek political philosophers and Augustine.

For an answer, we shall detour by way of Augustine's ontology and physics. Augustine, trained as a rhetor, had absorbed not only Plato and the Stoa, but also Aristotelian physics and metaphysics, then still considered one science. After his conversion he continued on the same course, having already laid his own philosophical foundation in a number of books written at Cassiciacum: *De beata vita, De ordine, Contra academicos, De pulchro et apto.*

One must remember, though, that he lived no longer in the Athens of 800 years ago but in the period of mature Hellenism. For several hundred years all philosophical endeavor had centered on the problem of God. The Stoics had deified the cosmos itself, Plotinus's God was "The One," to whom to ascend was every soul's desire. Aristotle's "Unmoved Mover" was still playing a role in cosmology. Where the philosophers seemed to have groped for an answer, Augustine supplied his from the first book of the Bible: *Deus creator omnium,* God is the creator of all things. From the Bible he also drew an answer regarding God's essence. God had revealed himself to Moses through the words: "I Am Who I Am." God is "I Am," the one whose essence is existence. Aristotle had attributed to God the origin of movement, Plotinus the essence of unity; Augustine perceived that God is the Existent who creates existing things out of nothing.

The biblical concept, admittedly received in faith, fitted smoothly into the traditional pattern of philosophical inquiry. "Of all visible things, the cosmos is the greatest; of all invisible, the greatest is God. That the world is, we see; that God is, we believe."[2] It served as an argument against the Stoics who had merged the created cosmos with its creator God. It answered, or rather, filled in, the theological gaps in Aristotle. Augustine found the biblical information, which he accepted on the authority of "witnesses," not less but rather better substantiated than the answer philosophers had attempted. In no wise could he see it in conflict with *scientia.* On the contrary, the insight

---

[2]Augustine, *The City of God* (Dods translation) XI, 4.

that things had been willed into existence by the good God brought to Augustine a new insight into these "things" and their nature. In all this, he never left the scope of the philosophical tradition, the inquiry into the rational intelligibility of given reality.

In another respect Augustine continued in the path of Greek philosophy while enriching it with elements of Christian revelation: knowledge was for him, as it was for Plato and Aristotle, a matter of "seeing" (*theōria*). He greatly widened and elaborated the derived notion of "inner vision," by means of which he overcame the argument of the skeptics about the unreliability of the senses. His original turn consisted in applying vision also to the highest good, in Christian terms, the "vision of God." One fully appreciates this when recalling that the sixteenth-century reformers, both Luther and Calvin, declared the ear to be man's most important organ for understanding. The object to be understood, of course, was the word of God which, according to Luther, should be "shouted not written" (*geschrien, nicht geschrieben werden*). That Augustine saved into the Christian doctrine the concept of *theōria* = "seeing" enabled him also to save the concept of the "nature" of things, which had historical consequences of immense importance. It continued to facilitate, well into modern times, an awareness of the givenness of the order of being, independently of human volition. One of the objections to this concept is that the "inner vision" tends to "see" what ought to be rather than what is. This particular objection, however, certainly does not apply to Augustine, as we shall find soon.

Augustine's ontology, centering on the hymn, "Deus creator omnium," was not merely the completion of Greek ontology by means of God, the Existent, as the creator of all that exists. It also answered the question of the relation between goodness and being more satisfactorily than it had ever been answered before. The ancient Greek tendency was to rely more on the clearly observable presence of purpose in existing things. A contemporary philosopher, Hans Jonas, has pointed to this feature in the following words: "In every purpose being opts for itself and against nothingness . . . *i.e.*, the mere fact that being is not indifferent toward itself establishes its difference from non-being as the value basis of all values, the first YES as such."[3]

Resting an ontology solely on observable purposefulness of existing things, however, causes that ontology to do less than justice to the vulnerability and endemic failure of being, *i.e.*, to "adversity." Augustine's ability to trace goodness to God the creator, however, not only facilitated his account of ontic adversity but also set up a court of highest instance, regarding goodness, above nature.

All these problems confront the modern reader with the difficulty that today we are lacking any ontology, so we have accustomed ourselves to an absolute cleavage between truth, the truth of indifferent facticity, on the one side, and goodness on the other. Still, in these matters Augustine is more approachable for the modern mind than others, precisely because Augustine, through his autobiography and his psychology, has anticipated many of the modern attitudes.

III

Augustine's theory of "adversity" has two dimensions. The first is the relative absence of perfection in things created from nothing. To begin with, Augustine changed Aristotle's notion of four grades of being:

> Among those beings which exist, and which are not of God's essence, those which have life are ranked above those which have none; those that have the power of generation, or even of desiring, above those which want this faculty. And, among the sentient, the intelligent are above those that have no intelligence. . . . And, among the intelligent, the immortal, such as the angels, above the mortal.[4]

---

[3]Hans Jonas, *Das Prinzip Verantwortung* (Frankfurt, 1979), p. 155.
[4]*City of God* X, 6 (hereafter cited only by book and chapter).

Next comes his concept of *minus esse*, less being, or being "contracted." This brought into his reach an intelligible accounting of the "adversities" through which created beings find themselves endemically threatened. It is important to remember that Augustine lived at a time when deep experiences of acute disaster and threat of annihilation had generated the monstrosity of the Gnostic religion, a radical way of explaining evil achieved by sacrificing any goodness in existing things, including man. It was clearly a case of throwing out the child with the bath. Many besides Augustine felt moved to call Gnosticism a monstrosity, which did not of itself enable them to come up with an alternative explanation.

Where Origen and Plotinus, who tried a philosophical refutation of Gnosticism, had themselves partly succumbed to it, Augustine succeeded brilliantly, helped above all by the notion of *creatio ex nihilo*, creation out of nothingness. Things created out of nothing lack the unlimited existence of God; they are, characteristically, "mutable." *Mutabilitas*, in this context, included the meaning of turning bad, a tendency to nothingness. Hence their need to "preserve such being as they have received."[5]

Aristotle's *soteria tou einai* is recalled, but with expanded scope and greater emphasis. God's creation is good, albeit subject to degeneration from being neither immutable nor immortal. Evil is a special case of mutability in creatures which have desire as well as intelligence. "For will, being a nature which was made good by the good God, but mutable by the immutable, because it was made out of nothing can both decline from good to evil, which takes place when it freely chooses, and can also escape the evil and do good; which takes place only with divine assistance."[6] This explanation of evil is capable of saving the concept of nature, which the Gnostics threw overboard in their anxiousness to account for extreme experiences of earthly misery. "It is not nature, but vice which is contrary to God. For that which is evil is contrary to the good. . . . Further the nature

---

[5]XII, 5.
[6]XV, 21 end.

it vitiates is a good, and therefore to this good it is also contrary
. . ."⁷

One should note the function of the term *vitium*: "Things
solely good, therefore, can in some circumstances exist; things
solely evil, never, for even those natures which are vitiated by an
evil will, in so far as they are vitiated, are evil, but in so far as
they are natures they are good."⁸ The noun, *vitium*, conveys at
the same time the ideas of fault, defect, and imperfection, so
that human misery can be accounted for by both *mutabilitas*
and *voluntas*, will.

Augustine's "reasonable" accounting of evil in a good creation has particular significance today. For we are living with the
painful experience of seeing the radical Gnostic doctrine of a
totally evil world, contrasted with the faraway reality of complete goodness, come back with social effectiveness, generating
the armed movements of modern totalitarianism. They serve as
a warning that philosophy cannot escape the responsibility of
explaining the anti-tendencies in the midst of things existing. A
naive theory of being, based on "seeing" things as they "ought
to be," cannot deliver a satisfactory explanation of "adversity"
and thus must fail in times of great historical and cultural catas-
trophes. Augustine's explanation, we note, does not disarm
nothingness but rather evil. Nothingness is a given possibility of
things created which, however, can be avoided with the help of
the good God, the ultimate Existent. Obviously, Augustine's
doctrine was opposed to all traditions of antiquity. If, nevertheless, the modern mind has hardly even taken cognizance of
Augustine's sophisticated analysis of adversity in human existence, the reason may possibly be found in a new philosophical
naiveté, the illusion of progress.

IV

Before turning to Augustine's ethics, we ought to throw a brief
glance at his anthropology. Having rejected the metaphysical

---

⁷XII, 3.
⁸*Ibid.*

dualism of the Manichees, but also that of Plotinus who placed opposite to God the equally eternal reality of matter, Augustine might have succumbed to the danger of a monism rooted in God as the sole existent. Augustine, however, emphatically renews the body-soul dualism of the Greeks, this time in the context of Christian revelation:

> What incredible thing it is, then, if some one soul is assumed by Him in an ineffable and unique manner for the salvation of many? Moreover, our nature testifies that a man is incomplete unless a body be united with a soul. This certainly would be more incredible, were it not of all things the most common; for we should more easily believe in a union between spirit and spirit, or, to use your own terminology, between the incorporeal and the incorporeal, even though the one were human, the other divine, the one changeable and the other unchangeable, than in a union between the corporeal and the incorporeal.[9]

Ontology is the backbone of Augustine's ethics, an ethics which he, by a stroke of genius, arranged in two columns. One column consists of accurate and detailed observations of the fallen human race, or, as Machiavelli would say, of "life as it is." The other column, however, is not "the ideal" as against "the real," but an equally empirical observation of god-centered human lives. Neither column consists of mere factual data: "When, therefore, man lives according to himself—that is, according to man, not according to God—assuredly he lives a lie . . ."[10]

Augustine describes the ways in which fallen man is a plaything of his lower passions, a being having lost the powers of self-control that were once his. "For what is man's misery but his own disobedience to himself."[11] Nor is his analysis to be misunderstood as a neo-Platonist contempt of the body in favor of the soul. The flesh, having been created by the good God, is not in itself evil. Rather, it is the evil will of the soul that causes

---

[9]X, 29.
[10]XIV, 11.
[11]XIV, 15.

the corruption of the creature as a whole. Augustine's analysis is as sophisticated as anything emerging from modern psychology, to which it is superior in that it has no need to invent a new and implausible myth.

The other column corresponds, in its function, to Aristotle's treatise on virtues, without, however, taking over Aristotle's confidence in the power of the virtues to do the "saving" job. For Augustine, the virtues have their place, but it is not at the top, for virtues may be resorted to by a will that, while yearning for goodness, is confident of being able to attain it by his own unaided efforts. The virtues of such a will Augustine calls "a perpetual war with vices—not other men's but our own."[12] The reason is that the will which does not cling to the living God has "no proper authority." It follows that

> the virtues which it seems to itself to possess . . . are vices rather than virtues as long as there is no reference to God in the matter. For although some suppose that virtues which have a reference . . . only to themselves are true virtues, the fact is that even then they are inflated with pride.[13]

The concept of will used in this analysis is a synonym for "love." "My love is my center of gravity" is the famous formula which Augustine frequently repeated. "The right will, therefore, is well-directed love, and the wrong will is ill-directed love."[14] Identifying will with love, Augustine is able to provide the needed affective element of ethics, which Aristotle found, not very convincingly, in man's love of the highest good not without also referring to man's love for the *nous*, "itself divine or only the most divine element in us."[15] In any case, Aristotle's loving affect is for an "it."

Augustine decisively improves on that by placing the love for the living God, a God addressed as "thou," at the center of the

[12]XIX, 4.
[13]XIX, 25.
[14]XIV, 7.
[15]Aristotle, *Nicomachean Ethics* X, 7.

good life. Through the channel of this love, divine grace, secured in Jesus Christ, will heal the defects of fallen human nature and enable man to retrieve the original goodness that created him. This, then, is the "supreme good," the ultimate happiness or, rather blessedness, for which man is destined, even though to get it he has to pass through the gateway of death, just as mankind has to complete the course of history. "There we shall enjoy the gifts of nature . . . not only of the spirit, healed now by wisdom, but also of the body renewed by resurrection."[16] Of this "ultimate consummation" a certain foretaste is possible even in this miserable life,

> when we have such peace as can be enjoyed by a good life. . . . Virtue, if we are living rightly, makes a right use of the advantages of this peaceful condition. . . . This is true virtue, when it refers all the advantages it makes a good use of, and all that it does in making good use of good and evil things, and itself also, to that end in which we shall enjoy the best and greatest peace possible.[17]

Or, again: "it is a brief but true definition of virtue to say, it is the order of love."[18]

V

Finally, we come to Augustine's political theory. Let us remember that Aristotle, having declared the *polis* the highest kind of human association, the one in which man finds it possible to live in "self-sufficiency," goes on to define the "true" forms of government, but then to study elaborately the "perverted" types characteristic of the world in which he lived. Now by contrast, Augustine had already drawn a full and chillingly "realistic" portrait of "the whole viciousness of human life," as he located

---

[16]*City of God* XIX, 10.
[17]*Ibid.*
[18]XV, 22.

the "perversion" not in political forms but in culture, the self-perpetuating pattern of habitual sinfulness.

The difference extends into the sociology of the two thinkers. Aristotle found in the "perverted" cities one unbridgeable social gulf, that between the rich and the poor, a gulf that allowed no common concept of justice to be perceived. Augustine's counterpart of that distinction is found in his "two cities." The term is misleading: I would prefer "two loyalties," or "two citizenries." The word *civitas* cannot mean "city" which certainly in antiquity would have meant a walled city with its own independent ruler. Augustine's two *civitates*, however, are neither living separately nor separately organized. They constitute groups readily observable in society who are distinct in terms of basic orientation and attitudes. Individual people, feeling drawn to each other by the love which they have in common, spontaneously form a group short of overt organization. In that sense, Augustine's two *civitates* resemble Aristotle's rich and poor. "The one consists of those who wish to live after the flesh, the other of those who live after the spirit; and when they severally achieve what they wish, they live in peace, each after their own kind."[19] Later, Augustine amplifies his distinction: "The former, in a word, glorifies in itself, the latter in the Lord. . . . The one lifts up its head in its own glory; the other says to its God, "Thou art my glory, and the lifter up of my head."[20]

The radical difference between Aristotle's and Augustine's observations at this point is that Aristotle's groups make government difficult or impossible, while Augustine's bear on the whole destiny of mankind. A further difference is that Augustine's two *civitates* have something basic in common with each other: the human need for peace in this mortal life. "The families which do not live by faith seek their peace in the earthly advantages of this life," while those who cleave to God "use as pilgrims such advantages of time and earth as do not fascinate and divert them from God."[21] Aristotle's rich and poor cannot

---

[19]XIV, 1.
[20]XIV, 28.
[21]XIX, 17.

coexist politically, unless there be a middle class to mediate. Augustine's two *civitates* share political order, albeit each for its own good: "As long as the two cities are commingled, we (*i.e.*, the City of God) also enjoy the peace of Babylon."[22]

VI

At this point, Augustine succeeds in creating a concept of a people that is compatible with historical contingencies. We are aware, of course, of what Aristotle said, in *Poetics* 1451 b, about the unbridgeable difference between philosophy and history, the former bound to statements of universals, the latter given only to "singulars." "By a universal statement, I mean one as to what such and such a kind of man will probably or necessarily say or do. . . ; by a singular statement, one as to what, say, Alcibiades did or had done to him." True to this separation, Cicero had defined a people as "an assemblage associated by a common acknowledgement of right and by a community of interests."[23]

Augustine shows forth the philosophical nature of this statement: Where there is no true justice there can be no right; so he concludes further that "where there is no true justice there can be no people," and that, according to Cicero, there could have been no Roman people. This difficulty disappears, however, when one defines a people as "an assemblage of reasonable beings bound together by a common agreement as to the objects of their love."[24] Peoples entertain multitudes of love, as fallen man does everywhere. An agreement on one of these loves constitutes a people. This is a concept of common culture as empirically created by common values. Contingent realities are here captured in a universal concept: such is the stuff of which philosophy of history is made. Later on, Ibn Khaldûn would add the notion of *asabiyah*, meaning "party spirit, team spirit, esprit

---

[22]XIX, 26.
[23]XIX, 17.
[24]XIX, 24.

de corps," a psychic element accounting for the genesis and decline of peoples.[25]

VII

The key concept of Augustine's political thought is peace. In book XIX, 11–17, he transforms Varro's idea of peace into one fitting the new ontology. The result is a complex of different tiers as well as kinds of peace, all of which are in some way related to each other. Through this complex run two main separating lines: eternal peace, ranking as an absolute above the merely relative earthly peace; and peace according to nature opposed as truth to the perverted unjust peace. Still, Augustine feels that there is room for a general remark: "We may say of peace, as we have said of eternal life, that it is the end of our good."[26] Earlier, Augustine has praised "blessedness," eternal felicity, as the highest destiny, not to be undone, for each particular person;[27] he now erects peace as the highest social good, and these two are merely the sides of the same coin. True peace will be ours only in eternal life.

Of peace on the earth Augustine speaks in such terms as "some peace," "peace of one kind or another," a "mere solace of our misery," "temporal peace." Still, even in the "misery" of this life, "peace is a good so great" that "there is no word we hear with such pleasure, nothing we desire with such zest, or find more thoroughly gratifying."[28] The language resembles that of Aristotle when talking about "happiness"; the shift of content is significant. All men desire to have peace with their own circle, Augustine observes. He might have added that even animals stake out their territory so as to keep their peace within defined

---

[25]Ibn Khaldûn, *The Muqaddhimah* (Princeton University Press, 1967); *cf.* also my *Between Nothingness and Paradise* (Louisiana State University Press, 1971), 180 ff.
[26]*City of God* XIX, 11.
[27]XII, 20.
[28]XIX, 11.

limits. Hence the reference to various groups and circles and "the laws of their own peace." The universal again permits referring to particulars, though not without reference to the absolute. The universal he has circumscribed in memorable words: "The peace of the body consists in the duly proportioned arrangement of its parts. The peace of the irrational soul is the harmonious repose of the appetites, and that of the rational soul the harmony of knowledge and action." One notes both, the Aristotelian concept of the soul, and the pervading concept of "nature" with its corollary, the "proper place" or "duly proportioned arrangement."

Augustine continues: "The peace of body and soul is the well-ordered and harmonious life and health of the living creature. Peace between man and God is the well-ordered obedience of faith to eternal law." What strikes us here is the effortless transition from Aristotelian metaphysics of "nature" to insights of Christian doctrine. But he is not finished:

> Peace between man and man is well-ordered concord. Domestic peace is the well-ordered concord between those of the family and those who obey. Civil peace is a similar concord among the citizens. The peace of the celestial city is the perfectly ordered and harmonious enjoyment of God, and of one another in God. Order is the distribution which allots things equal and unequal, each to its own place.[29]

As distinct from eternal peace, peace in this mortal life, as far as the godly citizenry is concerned, consists of "the use of things temporal with a reference to this result of earthly peace in the earthly community."[30] Earthly peace has the peculiar characteristic that it encompasses the two citizenries of mutually incompatible loyalties, the "earthly city" and the "City of God." "The things necessary for this mortal life are used by both kinds of men and families alike, but each has its own peculiar and widely differing aim in using them."[31]

---

[29]XIX, 13.
[30]XIX, 14.
[31]XIX, 17.

We note the emergence in Augustine's thought of an independent political function beyond and besides the mutually exclusive loyalties within the culture, the perception of an autonomous task of political rule. This was something at which Marx, much as he tried, never succeeded. Marx should be mentioned next to Augustine in this context, because like Augustine he considered the state a necessity brought about by the corruption of human nature, and therefore a temporary phenomenon.

God "did not intend that His rational creature, who was made in His image, should have dominion over anything but the irrational creation."[32] It is "sin which brings man under the dominion of his fellow." The state is necessary only because of men's vitiated natures, as is clear when just war must be waged because of "the wrong-doing of the opposing party."[33] Like Marx, Augustine delivers a scathing critique of society, its injustices, deceptions, discontents, and unreliabilities. Again, like Marx, he sees this world of sinful quarrels and dissensions not as man's true home. Those who live in faith, the "City of God," live "like a captive and a stranger in the earthly city." Yet, with hope in the highest promises of God and looking forward to true heavenly glory, they "make no scruples to obey the laws of the earthly city, whereby the things necessary for the maintenance of this mortal life are administered."[34] "Thus, as this life is common to both cities, so there is a harmony between them in regard to what belongs to it."[35] Still, the obligation to "obey the laws" of the state does not extend to that matter over which the two citizenries are most deeply divided, to divine worship.

Aristotle's supreme good of earthly happiness has become eternal blessedness beyond death and history. One wonders why Augustine might not be supremely disinterested in this world's political order, like Tertullian was before him. Augustine's ontological emphasis on existence, however, does not permit him to discount any existence, not even the most corrupted one.

---

[32]XIX, 15.
[33]XIX, 7.
[34]XIX, 17.
[35]*Ibid.*

Therefore he conceives of peace in two tiers: God's eternal peace, and relative peace on this earth, "such as we can enjoy in this life, from health and safety and human fellowship."[36] The relative peace includes:

> all things needful for the preservation and recovery of this peace, such as the objects which are accommodated to our outward senses, light, night, the air, and waters suitable for us, and everything the body requires to sustain, shelter, heal, or beautify it: and all under this most equitable condition, that every man who made a good use of these advantages suited to the peace of this mortal condition, should receive ampler and better blessings, namely, the peace of immortality.[37]

This is the counterpart of Aristotle's *soteria tou einai*, the preservation and protection of being in the security of the *polis*. Augustine, however, amends the concept, though not the activity, by pointing out that the real salvation of being can occur only in full union with God, after death. Remarkable, because Augustine acknowledges the legitimacy of earthly needs and their satisfaction; remarkable also because, in the nature of things, that cannot be the last word on the matter. In the "earthly city," where the relationship between earthly and eternal peace is ignored, that group "desires earthly peace for the sake of enjoying earthly goods, and it makes war in order to attain to this peace."[38] But, he adds, "as this is not a good which can discharge its devotees of all distress, this city is often divided against itself by litigations, wars, quarrels, and such victories as are either life-destroying or short-lived."[39] Or, to use Plato's words, because there are always those who live by evil loves, there "is no end of troubles," and human life cannot be ultimately preserved by any human political order. Still, Augustine is far from despising relative goods: "Miserable, therefore,

---

[36]XIX, 13.
[37]*Ibid.*
[38]XV, 4.
[39]*Ibid.*

is the people which is alienated from God. Yet even this people has a peace of its own which is not to be lightly esteemed."[40]

Is Augustine then an advocate of *any* kind of political order, as long as it exists? Would he side with Hobbes, or Machiavelli? He would not. First, having referred the relative to the absolute in an intelligible way, Augustine does allow for value gradations within the scope of the relatively good. Thus he says of the Romans, whose virtues he has sarcastically dismissed as "splendid vices," that "they were good according to a certain standard of an earthly state."[41] More important, though, he castigates the will to empire, which he attributes to certain men's proud wish "that all men belonged to them, that all men and things might serve one head, and might, either through love or fear, yield themselves to peace with him! It is thus that pride in its perversity apes God."[42] Within earthly imperfections, this peace, then, is still something that admits of intelligible distinctions, of grades of goodness, and of recognizable perversity.

VIII

That is all. No further concepts of political theory are in Augustine's bag. In particular: no explicit concept of the state, in terms of either genesis or covenant, nor any doctrine about forms of state. On the contrary, Augustine dismisses the problem: "The heavenly city (is) . . . not scrupling about diversities in the manners, laws, and institutions whereby earthly peace is secured and maintained."[43] Consequently, Augustine can see no point in a project to define or describe "the best state." Nor do offices and constitutional structure interest him. He never even mentions the rule of law. What he has to teach on war is not new. Revolutions are none of his concern. Thus, it hardly adds up to a systematic political theory. All the same, the way in

---

[40]XIX, 26.
[41]V,9.
[42]XIX, 12.
[43]XIX, 17.

which he puts politics in the total range of "things visible and invisible" provides important principles to guide discernment. What are his accomplishments?

One must recall the historical situation to get some of the answers. After those Church fathers who declared utter unconcern of Christians for the state, Augustine could declare: "The things which this city desires cannot justly be said to be evil, for it is itself, in its own kind, better than all other human good."[44] Not only is the state not unimportant, but among relative goods of this earth it holds top rank, so that Christians have a duty of loyal political participation. On the other side we find those Church fathers who saw in Rome's absorption of many smaller kingdoms a device of God to facilitate the spreading of the Christian Gospel. Foremost among them was Origen. After him, his disciple Eusebius had linked the *pax romana* to Christ's message of peace, so that he saw Constantine as completing a process that had begun with Christ and was continued by Augustus.[45] Here the Christian eschatology of old had turned into a proclamation of complete harmony between Christ and the Roman Empire. This consoling doctrine had been picked up by one Christian thinker after another.

Augustine, in turn, put a full stop to this thinking. Not only did he fail to praise Rome for its "contributions" to Christianity, he also deflated the expectation of an eventual Christian empire or kingdom. Of the Christian emperors, he treated Constantine with something like a polite bow[46] while heaping fulsome praise on Theodosius who had humbled himself before Ambrose. His historical prediction is by no means sanguine, for he looks for no more than sporadic appearances of this or that Christian ruler, rather than steady Christian progress.[47] Finally, one must not forget Augustine's severe prohibition of any speculation on a future millennium on the basis of Revelation

---

[44]XV, 4.

[45]*Cf.* Wilhelm Kamlah, *Christentum und Geschichtlichkeit* (Stuttgart, 1951), 175 ff.

[46]*City of God* V, 25.

[47]V, 21.

XX:4.[48] "At no time does Augustine leave the reasonable horizon of universals."[49]

Looking forward from Augustine, with the benefit of 20/20 hindsight, we observe that Eusebius, bypassing Augustine, as it were, stamped the influence of his imperial theology on the political thought of the Middle Ages. Augustine, in turn, also in a curious way, bypassed the Middle Ages and left his stamp, the stamp of typical Western autonomy, on Luther's faith as well as Descartes's reason. Beyond that, one might say Augustine's philosophy of history has come fully into its own only in the retrospection of modernity, just as Augustine's *Confession* was more deeply appreciated after the appearance of Western psychoanalysis. If Augustine left no systematic political thought in his time, there is, all the same, a Reinhold Niebuhr to testify to the long-range impulses of the fifth-century thinker. Niebuhr's witness certifies that Augustine, in an exemplary way, discharged the function of philosophy to criticize the illusory fascinations of the world with extant political structures and their pretenses.

IX

Finally, how about Augustine's concern for *soteria tou einai*, the preservation of man's being, its deliverance from "the troubles of the world"? This was our first, and fundamental question. It must be said, in all fairness to Plato and Aristotle, that Augustine did more and probed deeper to ascertain the nature and causes of these troubles. He traced them, partly through his ontology, partly through his ethics. Creatures are less perfect than their creator, and a tendency to nothingness is endemic to their existence. God has given them the power to perpetuate their kind, to heal themselves, even to correct their deficiencies. They are still subject to death and disease and, in the case of humans, to a basic corruption of their will. The human soul

---

[48]XX, 9.
[49]Kamlah, *op. cit.*, 320.

"has shown itself capable of being altered for the worse by its own will."[50] Hence the human race, that which is "nothing more social by nature," has become the most "unsocial by its corruption."[51] The *City of God* is filled with example after example of the truth of this statement, some taken from Roman history, others from sociological observation. Man, craving to become more than God, becomes less. That is Augustine's analysis which sees circumstances as symptoms of, rather than as causes for, human insecurity and discontent.

The analysis implies the remedy. Man's will has the power to change his nature for the worse but, once vitiated, it has no longer the power to restore itself. The good will is from God but not the evil will. Man, then, is saved only by regaining a closeness to God, but it is God who has opened that possibility once again. The way to the salvation of man's being goes necessarily through death, and resurrection, to an undisturbed enjoyment of the original goodness of his nature. The true blessedness, which is man's highest destiny, is not realized in history and in the world of history. Those who in hope of this destiny see themselves engaged in a "pilgrimage" can enjoy the peace of the heavenly kingdom in hope and in faith, while making, in a detached way, good use of the goods of this life.

While Augustine's emphasis lies on the otherworldly fulfillment, to which he devotes the last three books of his work, his most telling achievement is to have taken the state from the height of its pedestal. The state, administrator of the earthly peace which even in the most corrupt cases is "not to be lightly esteemed," has still the supreme authority, but that authority has none of the salvific elements that we find in Plato and Aristotle. Political order in this world, then, cannot be an "all-or-nothing" proposition. Salvation is of God, and, in this world, represented by those who have spiritual help to give. The limitation of the state's authority in favor of a spiritual order is obviously implied. Augustine is the intellectual father of the

---

[50]*City of God* XI, 22.
[51]XII, 27.

concept of the limited state, even though Pope Gelasius did provide the effective slogan. To this notion of a somewhat demoted secular power corresponds the other one: the concept of pilgrimage as the mold of historical continuity. Pilgrimage is an ongoing movement composed of many particular movements, yet not identical with any one nor with the sum of all. Pilgrimage is history's direction, its goal the peace of God, its attainment assured in Jesus Christ, its mood hopefully joyous. Pilgrimage is not progress; if anything, it is more akin to Hegel's dialectic, without the "self-movement." It is the human response to "the drawing of God's love and the calling of his voice," the response made in a social way, by a body of humans. Through this grand feature of a historical dynamism responding to God's healing grace, Augustine pulls together the threads of his ontology, ethics, politics, and history, a total movement toward the restoration of man's being.

A Covenant Theory of Personality:
A Theoretical Introduction

Paul C. Vitz

Dr. Paul C. Vitz, Professor of Psychology, New York University, attended the University of Michigan where he earned Phi Beta Kappa honors. He received his Ph.D. from Stanford University. He presently directs NYU's newly established graduate program in the psychology of art. Vitz's research into the relationship between Christian thought and the topics of personality theory, moral development, psychoanalysis, and counseling has produced such titles as *Psychology as Religion: The Cult of Self-Worship* and *Sigmund Freud's Christian Unconscious*. Vitz's latest book, *Modern Art and Modern Science: The Parallel Analysis of Vision*, reflects his scholarly interest in the relationships between contemporary aesthetics and science.

The concept of personality is central to much, perhaps even most, of psychology. The reason is that a theory of personality is really a theory about the nature of human nature. Hence, personality theory lies at the heart of all theories of psychotherapy and counseling. And, of course, through these applications, theories deeply affect the lives of countless individuals.

Now, the fundamentally religious nature of personality theory has long been recognized within psychology, but unfortunately, for an equally long period of time, this understanding has been pushed aside and neglected by psychologists active in the study and teaching of this important topic. Let us briefly review some of the evidence for the religious nature of personality theory.

Sigmund Freud, the originator of the first modern psychological theory of personality, wrote about psychoanalysis that it was not a branch of medicine; instead he described the psychoanalyst as a "secular pastoral worker . . ."[1] and psychoanalysis as "pastoral work in the best sense of the words."[2] It is also noteworthy that late in his life and rather plaintively, Freud commented, "I do not think our cures can compete with those of Lourdes. There are so many more people who believe in the miracle of the Blessed Virgin than in the existence of the unconscious."[3] Freud said many other things to make it clear that he understood psychoanalysis as having profound religious and theological significance,[4] but let us turn to other theorists. Carl Jung, for example, wrote: ". . . patients force the psychotherapist into the role of priest, and expect and demand of him that he shall free them from their distress. That is why we psychotherapists must occupy ourselves with problems which strictly speaking belong to the theologian."[5] One of Jung's best-known students, Jolande Jacobi, describes Jung's approach as follows:

> Jungian psychotherapy is . . . a Heilsweg, in the two-fold sense of the German word: a way of healing and a way of salvation. It has the power to cure . . . in addition it knows the way and has the means to lead the individual to his salvation, to the knowledge of and fulfillment of his personality, which have always been the aim of spiritual striving. Jung's system of thought can be explained theoretically only up to a point; to understand it fully one must have experienced or, better still, "suffered" its living action in oneself.
>
> Apart from its medical aspect, Jungian psychotherapy is thus a system of education and spiritual guidance.[6]

---

[1]Sigmund Freud, "Postscript to the Question of Lay Analysis" (1927), S.E. 20, Strachey, (Ed.), (London: Hogarth, 1959), p. 255.

[2]*Ibid.*, p. 256.

[3]"New Introductory Lectures on Psychoanalysis" (1933), S.E. 22, Strachey, (Ed.), (London: Hogarth, 1964), p. 152.

[4]See Paul C. Vitz, "Sigmund Freud's Attraction to Christianity: Biographical Evidence," *Psychoanalysis and Contemporary Thought*, 6:73–183 (1983); also Paul C. Vitz and J. Gartner, "Christianity and Psychoanalysis, Part I: Jesus the Anti-Oedipus" (1984). (Unpublished paper, read at the American Psychological Association Convention Meeting, Washington D.C., August 1982.)

[5]Carl Jung, *Modern Man in Search of a Soul* (New York: Harcourt, Brace, 1933), p. 278.

[6]Jolan Jacobi, *The Psychology of C. G. Jung* (New Haven, Conn.: Yale University Press, 1973), p. 60.

Now the process of Jungian movement on this path known as individuation is, Jacobi continues, "both ethically and intellectually an extremely difficult task, which can be successfully performed only by the fortunate few, those elected and favored by grace."[7] The last stage of the Jungian path, the goal, is called by Jung "self-realization."

The very similar, and now familiar, goal of "self-actualization" found in the theories of other psychologists, *e.g.*, Maslow,[8] is, of course, another case of the secular form of salvation. One might assume that by this time the essentially *religious* nature of the fundamental assumptions of any theory of the ideal personality would be generally recognized within psychology; such has not been the case. Indeed, if anything, personality theory is today more likely to be presented in a "scientific" context than it was when the secular approaches just mentioned were first being introduced years ago. The typical introductory psychology textbook begins with a definition of psychology as a science; then follow chapters on physiological and experimental psychology. Later—near the middle of the book—the subjects of personality, human motivation, clinical psychology, counseling, etc., are discussed—usually without any serious reconsideration of whether the original definition of psychology as a "science" is still defensible.

More advanced texts on these subjects emphasize somewhat less the scientific claim, but rarely, if ever, do they bring in any serious discussion of the profound religious, philosophical and moral implications of personality theory. It is not just that the religious foundations of these theories are omitted; even religious motivation as an important factor in the lives of millions of people is typically forgotten altogether. For example, take Salvatore R. Maddi's commonly used graduate text, *Personality Theories: A Comparative Analysis*,[9] which contains no reference to religious motivation anywhere in it. This text is espe-

---

[7]*Ibid.*, p. 127.

[8]Abraham H. Maslow, *Motivation and Personality*, 2nd ed. (New York: Harper and Row, 1970).

[9]Salvatore R. Maddi, *Personality Theories: A Comparative Analysis*, 3rd ed. (Homewood, Ill.: Dorsey, 1976).

cially informative, for its thorough coverage of the field of personality clearly exposes the neglect of religion by psychologists. The magnitude of psychology's oversight can be seen from the following: Maddi defines the core of personality as containing "the tendencies and characteristics that are present in all persons at all times, and that influence the directionality of life." Yet nowhere does Maddi, in all his 700-page summary of personality, suggest that religious motivation has any place in such a core. Even in his discussion of the *periphery* of personality, he leaves out all religious motivation. Finally, of course, Maddi nowhere examines the religious character of the assumptions of the secular theories which he does treat.

Sad to say, some of this anti-religious bias goes back to the first academic-research psychologist to propose his own theory of personality and motivation: Professor Henry Murray of Harvard who developed an approach which has been very influential in psychology — especially within academia. And his system is clearly quite hostile to Christianity in its basic formulations and categories. Unlike Freud and Jung, however, who acknowledged the theological implications of their work — Murray remained silent about the religious assumptions guiding his formulations.[10]

There has been some recent — and very effective — criticism of the anti-religious and other ideological biases of today's psychological theory.[11] The work from a Christian perspective of

---

[10]For more on this, see Paul C. Vitz, "A Christian Critique of Academic Personality Theory," *Studies in Formative Spirituality*, 3:263–282 (1982).

[11]Jay Edward Adams, *Competent to Counsel* (Nutley, N.J.: Presbyterian and Reformed Publishing Company, 1970); Gary P. Collins, *The Rebuilding of Psychology* (Wheaton, Ill.: Tyndale, 1976); Quintin R. DeYoung, "An Unknown God Made Known," *Journal of Psychology and Theology*, 4:87–93 (1976); Paul C. Vitz, *Psychology as Religion: The Cult of Self Worship* (Grand Rapids, Mich.: Eerdmans, 1977); Martin Bobgan and Deidre Bobgan, *The Psychological Way/The Spiritual Way* (Minneapolis: Bethany Fellowship, 1979); Donald MacCrimmon McKay, *Human Science and Human Dignity* (London: Hodder and Stoughton, 1979); Allen E. Bergin, "Religiosity and Mental Health: A Critical Reevaluation and Meta-analysis," *Professional Psychology: Research and Practice*, 14:170–184 (1983); William Kirk Kilpatrick, *Psychological Seduction* (Nashville, Tenn.:

Adams, Collins, DeYoung, Vitz, Bobgan and Bobgan, McKay, Bergin, and Kilpatrick has attracted serious attention. Likewise, the recent theoretical work of Bergin, Strong, and Vitz has begun to stimulate some new thinking in counseling and clinical psychology. From a strictly secular point of view, the ideological critiques of Szasz, Coan, Lasch, and many others are also starting to shake the old foundations. To this list I would like to add the recent — and I believe most significant works of two social psychologists, the first secular and the second Christian: Hogan and Van Leeuwen. With luck, this two-sided critical attack — from both Christians and secularists — will rudely but effectively awaken psychology from its religious, moral and philosophical slumber.

It would be possible to develop a book-length treatment of what might be called psychology's enormous intellectual scotoma, or blind spot, with respect to religion and related issues. But that would take us too far afield here. Suffice it to say that whatever blame for this problem lies with the ignorance, bias and self-interest of secular psychologists, it is probably matched by the passivity, intellectual cowardice and lack of imagination

---

Nelson, 1983); Allen E. Bergin, "Psychotherapy and Religious Values," *Journal of Consulting and Clinical Psychology*, 48:95–105 (1980); S. Strong, "Christian Counseling," *Counseling and Values*, 21:75–128 (1977); Paul C. Vitz, "From a Secular to a Christian Psychology," in P. Williamson and K. Perotta (Eds.), *Christianity Confronts Modernity* (Ann Arbor, Mich.: Servant Press, 1981); Paul C. Vitz, "A Christian Critique of Academic Personality Theory," *Studies in Formative Spirituality*, 3:263–282 (1982); Paul C. Vitz and J. Gartner, "Christianity and Psychoanalysis, Part 2: Jesus the Transformer of the Super-ego," unpublished paper (1984); Thomas Szasz, *The Myth of Mental Illness*, rev. ed. (New York: Harper and Row, 1974); Richard W. Coan, *Hero, Artist, Sage or Saint? A Survey of Views on What is Variously Called Mental Health, Normality, Maturity, Self-Actualization, and Human Fulfillment* (New York: Columbia University Press, 1977); Christopher Lasch, *Haven in a Heartless World: The Family Besieged* (New York: Basic Books, 1977) and *The Culture of Narcissism* (New York: Norton, 1979); R. T. Hogan and N. P. Emler, "The Biases in Contemporary Social Psychology," *Social Research* 45:478–534 (1978); R. T. Hogan and D. Schroeder, "The Joy of Sex for Children and Other Modern Fables," *Character* 1:1–8 (1980); Mary Stewart Van Leeuwen, *The Sorcerer's Apprentice: A Christian Looks at the Changing Face of Psychology* (Downers Grove, Ill.: Intervarsity, 1982).

on the part of the Christian intellectual community of the last few decades. (I should add that this double indictment most certainly includes the author, who has the dubious distinction of being guilty of both sets of charges: first as an atheistic secular psychologist for 20 years; and more recently as a Christian who far too often failed to speak out.)

But rather than criticize still further the secular psychologists, let us turn to the question: What might a Christian theory of personality be? Indeed, let us try to begin to answer this question, for it seems to me that the best way to criticize the secularists is to provide a concrete, Christian alternative. The best defense is, after all, a good offense — and it is much more fun besides.

The Christian Concept of Personality: General Assumptions and Characteristics

In fact, a Christian psychology is already emerging and it offers — already — the possibility of a real challenge to the secular stuff. And in the long run, I believe, it will be possible to "baptize" large portions of secular psychology: that is, to use what is valid in them, while removing their anti-Christian thrust. After all, if the threat of Aristotle to the faith could be dealt with by St. Thomas Aquinas, then there is hope that this newest expression of the Greek mentality can also be defused. In any case, something like this is absolutely needed, since psychology is here to stay. Unless a Christian model of psychology is found, Christianity will continue to lose millions of souls to the message of secular psychology.

Point One: Christian psychology is based on the assumption of the existence of God — specifically of a personal God. This point must be boldly stated not only to expose and challenge the hidden assumption of atheism existing in most contemporary psychology, but also to indicate from the outset that this assumption will have major positive implications for the concept of psychology. The acceptance of God enlarges and enriches psychology by seeing religious life as relevant and interpretable. The relationship between God and man—and, in particular, the nature of spiritual life—now become topics of discussion, topics in great need of understanding. But the existing secular and materialist psychology, to the extent that it is in fact valid, is no threat to a Christian psychology, any more than mathematics, physics, or biology are threats. And a sound Christian psychology will have to be built on a solid understanding of natural man, most especially of sinful or fallen man. So the first point to make is that a Christian psychology would, truly, be a psychology, but a bigger and better one than is currently available: a broader, deeper and truer psychology.

Now, this is not the place to take up the positive case for God, as it were, in the social sciences. But I will take up the case against the routine assumption of atheism—that is, the case against atheism in the social sciences. Here I can only sketch out a critique of the mythology of atheism in science by noting briefly some of the smaller myths or fabulations which serve to support it.[12]

Myth No. 1: Once a believer is exposed to modern intellectual life, he either becomes an atheist or an agnostic, or at least he becomes much less confident in the truth of religion. That is, the direction of modern intellectual change in "inevitably" from childish superstition to adult anti-religious rationality. Now some of my recent observations may be of interest in assessing this proposition. First, I am a convert, or more technically a re-convert to Christianity, after being a secular humanist and atheist for 20 years, roughly between the ages of 20 and 40. This has given me a special perspective on atheism but it has also put me in contact with a growing—and articulate—number of highly educated adult converts. As an example, in the past year or so I have been actively discussing the general issue of atheism and social science with a psychoanalyst, a sociologist, a social psychologist, and a brilliant young graduate student of clinical

---

[12]This critique is from Paul C. Vitz, "A Reply to Hogan and Schroeder," *Character* 1:4–5 (1980).

psychology—all of whom are recent converts. All of them are, moreover, actively working (writing, publishing) on the issue of the anti-religious bias in the social sciences. There are also many other examples in the academic world of recent conversions or returns to belief in God. In any case, it is a myth tied to the now-fading idea of a uni-directional notion of progress, which suggests that the only direction of change is from religion to irreligion—and never back again.

Myth No. 2: Belief in God is based on all kinds of irrational needs and wishes, but atheism is derived strictly from a rational, no-nonsense appraisal of the way things really are. Here, as a typical counter-example, I can again offer my own case history. I am not doing this to bore the reader with my life story, but to make clear that my reasons for becoming an atheist were largely without intellectual or moral integrity, and further, that these motives were, and still are, commonplace among social scientists. The major factors involved in my becoming an atheist (though I wasn't aware of them at the time) were as follows:

A. I wanted all impediments to my independence, to my ego, removed—thus my father and of course God had to go. This motivation, whether described as Oedipal wish-fulfillment or as a desire for autonomy (*i.e.*, narcissistic control of my future life) makes little difference, since beliefs serving such motives are easily understood as self-serving.[13]

B. I wanted to escape my father and my family in a social sense as well. I was vaguely embarrassed to be from the Midwest, for it seemed terribly dull, narrow, and provincial. There was certainly nothing romantic about being from Cincinnati, Ohio, and from a vague German-English background. Terribly middle class. Thus, besides escape from a dull and, according to me, unworthy past, I wanted—like so many of my classmates—to escape my somewhat embarrassing social, ethnic and religious background.

---

[13]For a detailed critical analysis of the neurotic irrational bases for Freud's atheism, see Paul C. Vitz and J. Gartner, "Christianity and Psychoanalysis, Part 1: Jesus the Anti-Oedipus," unpublished paper (1984). (Paper read at the American Psychological Association Convention Meeting, Washington, D.C., 1982.)

C. A final reason for my wanting to become an atheist was that I desired to be accepted by the powerful and influential scientists in the field of psychology. In becoming a psychologist I was joining a new group, and of course I became socialized in the process. Just as I learned to dress like a typical college student by putting on the right clothes, I also learned to think like a proper psychologist by putting on the right—read: atheistic—ideas and attitudes.

In short, for the needs of my ego, for my social needs, and for my professional career needs, atheism was simply the best policy. Looking back on these motives, I can honestly say that a return to atheism has all the appeal of a return to adolescence.

Myth No. 3: Religion is slowly (or rapidly) disappearing. Throughout the modern period, the assumption has often been made—either directly or tacitly. At present, as the modern period is ending, and a still ambiguous post-modern period starts, this assumption looks increasingly problematic. In this country, in Africa, in India and much of the rest of Asia, in South America, even in Russia—and certainly in the Muslim world—religion is alive and well. Indeed, the three most influential leaders in the world—Pope John Paul II, Alexander Solzhenitsyn, and the Ayatollah Khomeini—all derive their influence, for good or ill, from a religious base. There are many other signs which could be mentioned, of the continued general health of religion in this country and elsewhere. In short, this myth of the imminent demise of religion should be seen as the secular wish-fulfilling prophecy that it is.

Myth No. 4: Reason in the form of rational argument and proof overwhelmingly supports the position of atheism. This myth is a holdover from the now widely discredited positivistic philosophy that has strongly influenced most graduate education in social science, at least for the past fifty years. In fact, the statement "God does not exist" is, of course, impossible to prove: it is logically equivalent to the absurdity of trying to prove the null hypothesis. If one backs off into agnosticism or skepticism, one is in the familiar but psychologically pathetic limbo of having to accept the null hypothesis—which means that it is possible that God, and his morality, do exist. Certainly social scientists in this state of uncertainty should be much less confident of — much less smug in — their atheism than they have tended to be. More to the point, perhaps, recent powerful arguments using the latest tools of rationalistic philosophy are now providing very important support for the theistic position. Here the works of Plantinga, Ross, Swinburne and others are especially significant.[14] My experience with atheists in social science is that they have never even heard of these men, much less read them. In the great majority of cases, this means that the atheism of today is based on a woefully outdated, and in any case, poorly understood philosophy. As a result, it is news to most social scientists that God is *not* dead — but that Bertrand Russell *is*.

Point Two: A Christian psychology (at least an orthodox one!) comes with a clear and well-worked-out morality and value system. Now, every psychology, most especially any form of psychotherapy, always has a value system and a concept of morality. This issue cannot be avoided. The great problem with the present secular psychologists is that, although they do acknowledge the inevitability of value systems, they have not clearly stated what theirs *is*.

Further, if secular psychologists did explicate their value system, it would become clear to all that their values are often *ad hoc*, frequently extremely inconsistent — and often at odds with the values of their patients.[15] The most common value system seems to be of a permissive, relativist type. Whatever can be said in favor of relativism (and there is relatively little), I don't think it has ever been a functioning ethical system in any society

[14]Alvin Plantinga, *God and Other Minds* (Ithaca, N.Y.: Cornell University Press, 1967) and *The Nature of Necessity* (Oxford: Oxford University Press, 1979); James F. Ross, *Philosophical Theology* (Indianapolis: Bobbs-Merrill, 1969) and *Portraying Analogy* (Cambridge: Cambridge University Press, 1981); Richard Swinburne, *The Coherence of Theism*, *The Existence of God*, and *Faith and Reason* (Oxford: Oxford University Press, 1977, 1979, 1981).

[15]For a discussion of this issue, see Allen E. Bergin, "Psychotherapy and Religious Values," *Journal of Consulting and Clinical Psychology* 48:95–105 (1980).

for more than a few decades at most. Relativism is simply based on so much sand that its incoherence soon destroys those who live by it. But Christian values and morality, which are similar to many other traditional moral systems, are clear, familiar to many, and, outside "intellectual" circles, generally held in high esteem. A clearly specified moral system thus gives to a Christian psychology—announced as such—a significant advantage over the various competing, covert secular value systems.

We should note here one further aspect of crucial importance about psychology assuming, from the start, the nonexistence of God. In the past 30 years, there has been a great deal of evidence for the accuracy of Dostoevsky's remark: "If God does not exist, then anything is permitted." In certain respects God can be thought of as the gold standard when it comes to morality: a much-needed reference point in these days of inflated, relativistic secular thought. I realize, of course, that for the members of today's academic establishment, God—like gold—is not a reality, but a kind of barbarous relic.

This question of moral values brings me to yet another—a fifth—myth about atheistic psychology.

Myth No. 5: Reason plus experience can arrive at a viable moral system. Now this may be possible, but the history of attempts to arrive at a philosophic or scientific ethic (lacking a theistic core) hardly gives rise to much confidence on this score. One powerful reason for this is that no one has found how to get from what *is* to what *should* be. The gap between the realms of "is" and "should" appears rationally and empirically unbridgeable. The fact is that the living and functioning moral systems in the world today are all rooted in religion—typically in the belief in God—*e.g.*, Jewish, Christian, Islamic morality. It is also of interest that the core morality of these religions—and of others around the world—is essentially the same.

Even if a rationalistic ethic is possible, it remains true that the great majority of intelligent discussion about the moral life has been produced by wise rabbis, great Christian theologians and Muslim scholars. Certainly these contributions should not be written out of the debate, as if they were "fairy tales," by social scientists grappling with moral issues. I hope that as psychology breaks new ground, it will also break the longstanding taboo against reference to God and to religiously based moral argument in the social sciences.

This clash over moral interpretations can be clearly seen by a summary of how theistic psychotherapy would differ in its values from today's secular humanistic approach as shown in Table I. This table, with a few minor changes, is taken from an important article by Professor Allen Bergin,[16] a devout Mormon and prominent clinical psychologist who has recently acknowledged the great relevance of religion for understanding psychotherapy.

Point Three: A Christian psychology introduces fundamental new concepts and practices into psychology and counseling. For example, many types of prayer have been used by various Christian psychologists as part of their therapy. Fasting — another time-honored Christian practice — has been found useful. And whatever healing takes place is understood to occur as the result of the action of the Holy Spirit, and credit is not taken by the therapist. Indeed, the invoking of the power of the Holy Spirit — a major factor in Christian counseling — is unique to it; and the dramatic changes reported often make traditional psychotherapy look pretty inadequate.

Of perhaps even greater interest are specifically Christian psychological concepts which can greatly enrich an understanding of psychological change. For example, take the notion of forgiveness, an idea central to the Christian life. Although forgiveness is a powerful force for healing, no secular theory of psychology mentions, much less uses, forgiveness. After all, in the secular world of the ego, to forgive is a sign of weakness. (Indeed, learning to be *angry* at others is what most of "consciousness-raising" is all about: one comes to an awareness of how badly one has been treated by others! Forgiveness has no role here!) In secular therapy one is to *forget* — but not *forgive*. The irony is that it is not really possible to forget, but it is

---

[16]*Ibid.*

Table I
Theistic Vs. Clinical Vs. Humanistic Values
(from Bergin, 1980, p. 100)

Theistic	Clinical-Humanistic
1. God is supreme. Humility, acceptance of (divine) authority and obedience (to the will of God) are virtues.	1. Man is supreme. The self is aggrandized. Autonomy and rejection of external authority are virtues.
2. Personal identity is eternal and derived from the divine. Relationship with God defines self-worth.	2. Identity is ephemeral and mortal. Relationships with self and others define self-worth.
3. Self-control, in terms of absolute values. Strict morality. Universal ethics.	3. Self-expression, in terms of relative values. Flexible morality. Situation ethics.
4. Love, affection and self-transcendence primary. Service and self-sacrifice central to personal growth.	4. Personal needs and self-actualization primary. Self-satisfaction central to personal growth.
5. Committed to marriage, fidelity and loyalty. Emphasis on procreation and family life as integrative factors.	5. Open marriage or no marriage. Emphasis on self-gratification or recreational sex without long-term responsibilities.
6. Personal responsibility for own harmful actions and changes in them. Accept guilt, suffering and contrition as keys to change. Restitution for harmful effects.	6. Others responsible for our problems and changes. Minimize guilt and relieve suffering before experiencing its meaning. Apology for harmful effects.
7. Forgiveness of others who cause distress (including parents) completes the therapeutic restoration of self.	7. Acceptance and expression of accusatory feelings is sufficient.
8. Knowledge by faith and self-effort. Meaning and purpose derived from spiritual insight. Intellectual knowledge inseparable from the emotional and spiritual. Ecology of knowledge.	8. Knowledge by self-effort alone. Meaning and purpose derived from reason and intellect. Intellectual knowledge for itself. Isolation of the mind from the rest of life.

possible to forgive. In a word, forgiveness, with its many benefits for the psyche (and the soul) has no place in any secular
approach to psychotherapy or counseling.

Closely related to the issue of forgiveness is the notion of
responsibility for our actions — and above all taking responsibility for our harmful actions, even if we felt justified in hurting,
hating, or striking back at another. This important idea has
been especially well discussed by the Christian psychologist
Stanley Strong.[17] It is worth noting that in its emphasis on
responsibility, a Christian psychology can make use of certain
secular psychologies — such as, for example, aspects of Glasser's
reality theory.[18]

There is an ancient and honorable Christian "trait theory" of
personality which has much to recommend it, and which could
easily be developed within a modern psychological context:
namely, the description of personality in terms of virtues or
characteristics: faith, hope, charity, or love. (This last
concept — Christian charity — especially needs to be substituted
for what passes for love in the humanist tradition.) And also the
cardinal virtues of prudence, justice, temperance and courage.
Other religious virtues: patience, chastity, humility, etc., need
to be rediscovered and studied by theoreticians of personality.

Finally there is much to be learned about the psychology of
suffering and the ways in which suffering can lead to the growth
of personality. It is the *de*construction of the ego and experiences which might be called "ego-stripping" which are the keys
to the highest level of personality. For the Christian this raises
the psychology of "taking up the cross" and of such after all
remarkable comments as "I must decrease and He (Christ) must
increase." In short, even this brief treatment should make clear
the many new practices and concepts that exist within the Christian tradition.

Point Four: A Christian psychology is an interpersonal psychology. It is first of all Christ-centered, and then other-

---

[17]Stanley Strong, "Christian Counseling," *Counseling and Values* 21:75–128
(1977).
[18]William Glasser, *Reality Therapy* (New York: Harper and Row, 1965).

centered. The two great commandments encapsulate this fundamental Christian approach most powerfully. That is, for
Christianity, one's personality is developed and grows out of a
relationship with others—the most important "other" being
Christ Himself. This emphasis is, of course, in striking contrast
to the many secular theories, which all identify the autonomous
self, the consciously cultivated independent ego, as the central
focus of personality development.[19]

But to get some real sense of what a Christian psychology
would be like, we can perhaps do no better than to look at two
major Christian writers, one a Catholic and one a Protestant,
both of whom introduced the case for a Christian concept of
personality at about the same time, forty years ago. As far as I
can discover, no psychologist has—thus far—taken up their
suggestions. First, here is the statement of Dietrich von Hildebrand, in his *Liturgy and Personality*:

> To die to ourselves in order that Christ may live in us, is thus the
> only path leading to full personality in a far truer sense of the
> word; and it is this path which is open through the grace of God
> even to those who possess only a humble natural "essential
> endowment." This dying to oneself, does not, however, mean the
> giving up of individuality. On the contrary, the more a man
> becomes "another Christ," the more he realizes the original
> unduplicable design of God which this man represents . . .[20]

Hildebrand goes on to note:

> Nevertheless, it should be held in mind that it would be a great
> mistake to place before ourselves the aim of becoming personali-
> ties in this higher sense. . . . However high the value attached to
> the participation in the breadth and fullness of God, the words
> of Christ can be applied to is: "Seek ye first the kingdom of God
> and his justice, and all these things shall be added unto you."

---

[19]For example, see Michael A. Wallach and Lise Wallach, *Psychology's Sanction for Selfishness: The Error of Egoism in Theory and Therapy* (San
Francisco: Freeman, 1983).

[20]David von Hildebrand, *Liturgy and Personality* (New York: Longmans
Green, 1943), pp. 33–34.

In different words the Anglican C. S. Lewis, in *Beyond Personality*, makes a remarkably similar claim about the Christian concept of personality:

> The more we get what we call "ourselves" out of the way and let Him take over, the more truly ourselves we become. . . . In that sense our real selves are all waiting for us in Him. It is no good trying to "be myself" without Him. The more I resist Him and try to live on my own, the more I become dominated by my own heredity and upbringing and surroundings and natural desires. In fact what I so proudly call "Myself" becomes merely the meeting place for trains of events which I never started and which I cannot stop. What I call "my wishes" become merely the desires thrown up by my physical organism or pumped into me by other men's thoughts or even suggested to me by devils. Eggs and alcohol and a good night's sleep will be the real origins of what I flatter myself by regarding as my own highly personal and discriminating decision to make love to the girl opposite to me in the railway carriage. Propaganda will be the real origin of what I regard as my own personal political ideals. I am not, in my natural state, nearly so much of a person as I like to believe: most of what I call "me" can be very easily explained. It is when I turn to Christ, when I give myself up to His Personality, that I first begin to have a real personality of my own.[21]

Lewis also adds the same qualification as von Hildebrand:

> But there must be a real giving up of the self. You must throw it away "blindly" so to speak. Christ will indeed give you a real personality: but you must not go to Him for the sake of that. As long as your own personality is what you are bothering about you are not going to Him at all. The very first step is to try to forget about the self altogether. Lose your life and you will save it. Submit to death, death of your ambitions and favourite wishes every day and death of your whole body in the end: submit with every fibre of your being, and you will find eternal life. Keep back nothing. Nothing in you that has not died will

---

[21]C. S. Lewis, *Beyond Personality* (London: Bles, 1944), pp. 63–64.

ever be raised from the dead. Look for yourself, and you will find in the long run only hatred, loneliness, despair, rage, ruin, and decay. But look for Christ and you will find Him, and with Him everything else thrown in.

A. The Origin of the Concept "Person"

To further develop the basis for a Christian concept of personality, let us consider some important historical background taken largely from Müller and Halder. As many psychologists know, the word "person" comes from the Latin "persona" which means mask, and also the theatrical role that went with the mask. (The Latin was probably first used as the best equivalent to a Greek word with the same meanings.) But the origins of the word "person" is not a significant thing: what *is* important is that the *concept* of a "person" which is unique to the Western world was first introduced into Western thought as part of basic Christian theology. That is, the first use of the word for person in the modern sense arose out of the theology of the Trinity and of the Incarnation: God as three persons, and Christ as both the second person of the Trinity and as its perfect embodiment in human form. Now, of course, in certain respects, the origin of the idea of a person is found in Judaism, in which, from the beginning, God was understood as a person, and not merely as an abstraction. Yahweh was a personal God. But in any case, the concept of a person "remained unknown to ancient pagan philosophy and first appears as a technical term in early Christian theology . . ."[22] The concept of a "person" then continued to develop within the framework of Christian thought, for hundreds of years—and this concept of a person "still determines modern thinking to a great extent."[23]

The notion of personality in its contemporary psychological and utterly secular sense is quite recent, being no more than fifty or sixty years old. In view of the anti-theistic character of

---

[22]M. Müller and A. Halder, "Person: Concept," in *Sacramentum mundi*, Volume 4 (New York: Herder and Herder, 1969), p. 404.
[23]*Ibid*.

modern personality theory it is not surprising that these secular theories should end up by reducing the concept of a person to something like the pre-Christian pagan idea: that is, to an essentially naturalistic idea of an *individual*. As we will see, the concept of a person and that of an individual are in many respects opposites. The pagan notion of an individual, for example, is lacking the dignity and spiritual dimension of the Judeo-Christian understanding of a person, which always implies, necessarily, that one is a person because he or she is made in the image of God. Indeed, the widespread loss of respect for the person in recent decades — as in abortion, pornography, fascism, etc. — can be attributed, in part, to the rise in prominence of the secular, modern pagan understanding of "personality" (really individuality) — which has no concept of our sacred nature.

B.   A "Covenant Theory" of Personality

The point of this history is not just to identify the strongly Christian origin of the notion of person, but primarily to show its direct relevance to a concept of Christian personality which has yet to be explored by psychology — at least by modern psychology. The general situation can be summarized thus: Each human being is created in the image of God; true personality is the expression of this image, or divinely implanted "role," if you will; expression requires that the person attend to, and respond to, God — that is, each of us must love and cooperate with God. For the Christian this means loving and following — imitating — Jesus, who as the perfect incarnation of God gives us the model for expressing our latent, true personality. The fact that God was incarnate and dwelt among us gives the Christian the unique and enormously beneficial model of Jesus with whom to identify. The process of identifying with Jesus has both psychological and spiritual aspects to it.[24] The psychological aspects of

---

[24]Paul C. Vitz, *Sigmund Freud's Christian Unconscious* (New York: Guilford, 1984) (in press).

this religious centering of personality are available for study, and some of these have been noted earlier; many of the spiritual aspects, although intrinsically unavailable for study and experiment, have effects that can be readily observed—and can be contrasted with purely psychological characteristics. Psychology has learned to live with the mind-body problem, and it can learn to live with what might be called a mind-spirit problem as well.

The other, closely related, great interpersonal emphasis of a Christian theory of personality is the concern with, the love of, others; that is, the concern with committed or covenant relationships with others. The central psychological principle here is that personality is developed into its highest form through loving commitment to others. It is through *caritas*: through serving others—even unto death—that the Christian personality grows and reaches its highest development. The very idea of commitment, of deep caring for another, of being bonded to another, is the exact opposite of so much of today's humanistic psychology. Today nothing must hinder the growth of the ego; nothing—no one—must restrict the autonomy of the individual. Perhaps James Bond of movie fame is the best example of this ideal—a man without any bonds with anyone. He appears to have no mother or father, no true friends; and certainly the whole idea of his relationship with women is to avoid commitment. Hugh Heffner is another familiar example of this kind of "personality." The idea that a man's personality is developed— "created," if you will—by bonds of commitment to others, is antithetical to all of contemporary personality theory.[25]

C.   The Concept of "Covenant" and the Origin of Personality

I begin this brief outline of covenant theory by noting, again, that each human being is created in the image of God and that becoming a person, that is, developing our personality, is the expression of this divinely implanted image.

---

[25]For a book-length documentation of this claim see Michael A. Wallach and Lise Wallach, *Psychology's Sanction for Selfishness: The Error of Egoism in Theory and Therapy* (San Francisco: Freeman, 1983).

In creating a person God initiates a covenant with him or her. The very bringing of a person into existence is a demonstration of God's covenant love; God begins the relationship of covenant and asks that we reciprocate: we are each to love God and to love others (the two great commandments). We are to love God because He loves us, and we are to love others because God loves them — even if they don't love us, *e.g.*, our enemies. The essence of covenant, then, is committed agape love, and it can be characterized by showing faithfulness, hope, loyalty, patience, courage, and related psychological characteristics. The presence of these "virtues" should be seen as evidence that a person has developed, that one is expressing the image of God — the person — implanted in us.

Now God gives each of us the choice to freely choose to covenant with Him. We are constantly offered the choice to reaffirm our commitment to God and others or to reject covenant. Since Adam we have reliably chosen to reject God and to choose ourselves, that is, various idols which are disguised projections of the self. This fundamental tendency based on pride creates the pervasive human expression of narcissism, that is, the choice of self-love over love of God and others. (This is, of course, the familiar, fundamental motivation of Satan.) The scandal of modern psychological theory is that it openly champions the narcissistic love of oneself and explicitly rejects love of God and of others. (Some, like Fromm, deny this but in fact their denial is only superficial, since the proposed love of others is always dependent on a prior, total commitment to the self and its desires. The individual self is always the final, ultimate court of approval. Fromm, in spite of his occasional protests against selfishness and narcissism, proposed a theory that is thoroughly based on self-love with all its destructive consequences.)[26]

Because men chose, in general, to break the covenant with God, the Jews were explicitly chosen to keep the covenant alive.

---

[26]Erich Fromm, *The Art of Loving* (New York: Harper, 1956). See Paul C. Vitz, *Psychology as Religion: The Cult of Self-Worship* (Grand Rapids, Mich.: Eerdmans, 1977); William Kirk Kilpatrick, *Psychological Seduction* (Nashville, Tenn.: Nelson, 1983); Wallach and Wallach, *ibid*.

And, the history of the Jews has been a constant struggle with the powerful tendency to break this covenant, to run after false gods, all "disguised" projections of the self. (Examples of the substitute for Jehovah range from Astarte and Baal to secular Zionism.) This covenant with the Jews is God's first explicit social covenant and by implication there is a Jewish covenant psychology—that is, a psychology of how a Jew is to express his or her internal image of God. This "old" or first covenant theory of personality would presumably derive from the history of the struggle to express, maintain, and develop the covenant that God made with the Jews, a story centered on the great Jewish figures such as Abraham, Moses, Joseph, David, and the prophets—all models for a covenant psychology.

However, the present focus is on the New Testament or New Covenant, which is understood as completing and fulfilling the original covenant—but certainly not negating it. In this new covenant all people have been given Jesus as the model for a covenant relationship with God and with others. The image of God in us—the person in us—develops through a commitment with Jesus and others. It is through this loving commitment to others that each human being comes into a fuller existence as a person—that is how one "becomes a person."

When Carl Rogers titles his well-known book *On Becoming a Person*,[27] he is simply wrong. Instead he has written a book on becoming an *individual*, in particular, an autonomous, self-actualizing, independent individual. An individual is created by separating from others, by breaking, by concentrating psychological energy and affect on the self instead of on God or others. The founders of modern psychology clearly knew this. The first expression of the ideas Rogers made more widely known is in the earlier writings of Alfred Adler and Carl Jung. Adler called his psychology "Individual Psychology"; Jung called the central process of self-development "individuation." Hence, Rogers should have called his book *On Becoming an Individual*. But a person is in fundamental respects the opposite of an

---

[27]Carl Rogers, *On Becoming a Person* (Boston: Houghton Mifflin, 1962).

individual, for a person comes into existence by connecting with others—not by separating, by choosing covenant and connection, not by choosing autonomy and separation. That is, much of humanistic self-psychology is the anti-psychology or anti-structure of a Christian covenant psychology. (Philosophy has long maintained the difference between the individual and the person, *e.g.*, Maritain.[28])

For example, in our relationship to others, Christians are called to love and to forgive while secular psychology calls people to trust and to forget. Briefly, let us look at these relationships. First, one should ask whether it makes any sense to make trust in others the fundamental virtue. Certainly not—and Jesus never asks one to do it. (He was too much of a Jewish realist.) Jesus certainly never trusted others; in particular, he didn't trust the apostles and for good reason, since one would betray him, another deny him, and all abandon him. But he did love them! A mother may not always trust her child, a husband may not always trust his alcoholic wife, but both can always love. After one has been betrayed once, much less long before "seventy times seven," one would be a fool to trust the other person—but it is still possible to forgive. Secular psychology is being utterly foolish to ask to trust, much less to forget, under the circumstances. In short, to love and when hurt to forgive is realistic and possible (however difficult), but to trust and when hurt to forget is foolish and impossible. (It is impossible to truly forget that another has hurt you.)

One further major point that distinguishes a Christian and covenant theory of personality from a secular and self theory of the individual: A covenant theory is not just psychologically realistic, it is based on reality—on that which exists outside of the self. To become a person is to be respectful of external realities. All secular theories of personality, by making the self the center of personality, in contrast, withdraw one from reality, from the external world created by God and filled with real

---

[28]Jacques Maritain, *The Person and the Common Good* (Notre Dame, Ind.: Notre Dame Press, 1966).

others. In short, secular theories of the individual are intrinsically subjective. This means that the secular psychology of a person is intrinsically relativistic and tends to solipsism, nihilism, and total subjectivism. The good example of this tendency is Carl Rogers's most recent book in which he argues for a thoroughgoing subjectivism: "there are as many realities as there are persons"; — we must prepared for a world of "no solid basis, a world of process and change . . . in which the mind . . . creates, the new reality."[29] Other evidence for the subjectivity of much "personality" theory has been its reliable tendency to merge with Eastern religion, with subjective drug states and many kinds of occult world views that claim reality is the creation of each self. The ultimate narcissism is that you are the creator of the world. For a discussion of this tendency of self and individual-oriented psychology to turn into subjectivism, see Kilpatrick.[30]

Actually, the essential logic of becoming an individual — that is, of separating and distancing the self from others — eventually gets carried to its logical extreme. First you break the "chains" that link you to society, then to others, then the chains that link you to self, and finally, the rejection of the self itself — that is, separation from the illusion of the ego, culminating in an experience, or state of nothing. Radical autonomy finally means separation from everything, it means total or ultra autonomy where the self is gone, hence, the affinity of self-psychology for transpersonal psychology and finally the subjective states of various Eastern religions.

The development of a person, being the anti-process of the "development" of an individual, moves in an opposite direction. The person is created by union with God and others. It is love that brings this union — this enlargement. The person knows not the "peace of nothing" — but instead knows the joy of union in love. We are one with Christ — and Christ and the Father are one.

---

[29]Carl Rogers, *A Way of Being* (Boston: Houghton Mifflin, 1980), p. 352.
[30]William Kirk Kilpatrick, *Psychological Seduction* (Nashville, Tenn.: Nelson, 1983).

D.   Manhood and Fatherhood, Womanhood and Motherhood
     as Basic to a Person

Still more explicitly we are called to become a man or a
woman — "male and female He created then." After our existence, our sex is the basic reality. Thus, a covenant psychology
leads directly to the psychology of manhood and womanhood
(something no secular self-psychology has ever mentioned).

As just one example of this expression of covenant psychology, we take the great and traditional interpersonal relationship
of father to son or daughter. To my knowledge, there is no
theory of personality or psychotherapy which has as a central —
or even as a peripheral premise — that a man's personality is
nourished and brought to richness, strength and deep significance, through being a father. This absence — aside from being
profoundly anti-social — is intellectually inexcusable. One has
only to look at the greatest works of literature to see how
important to humanity the themes of fatherhood and sonhood
have been. We in the West have become a people — a society —
with no concept of fatherhood. Our theories of what it means
to be a man, a male person, contain no reference to fatherhood.
Is it any wonder that we are also a nation of absent fathers? But
Christianity has always known the importance of fatherhood —
and I don't just mean the biological relationship. Christian history is full of men, from St. Paul to Chuck Colson, who developed as Christians — as distinctive "persons" — in large part
through their very functioning as *fathers* to others.

The same goes, of course, for motherhood. I began with a
discussion of the importance of fathers, because it is that relationship which seems in such danger of collapse at present. But
even that greatest of all human commitments — motherhood —
the covenant between mother and child — has been very much
undermined in recent years. Again, one looks in vain, in our
psychologies of personality, for theory which places *any* emphasis on being a mother as central to the development of a mature,
deep personality in a woman. And again, the Christian emphasis on the relationship of mother to child is not restricted to

marriage, or to biological motherhood. From Mary and Martha in the New Testament to Mother Teresa of Calcutta, Christian history is filled with great "mothers" who had no natural children.

The best that the secular theories can come up with is the notion of a "parent," with its verb, "to parent." Such uni-sex categories, such neutering of human identity — of archetypes — should be seen as the lifeless abstractions that they are — fit only for bureaucrats and for social science texts. Away with them! They belong with all those who see having a son or daughter as hampering their androgynous "self-fulfillment" . . .

Looking back, I think we can see that the various points mentioned and commented upon briefly provide a general structure of a Christian theory of personality which could easily be developed more fully. No doubt, within the different Christian traditions there would be different emphases — but the essential ideas are clear. It only remains for us Christians to get off our behinds and to break the anti-religious silence in psychology by developing our rich theological heritage with its fundamental understanding about the ultimate nature of personality.

The first official installment of much of the Christian approach to personality described here was given as the Neil C. McMath Lectures for 1981 at the School of Theology, Detroit, Michigan, October 31, 1981. Subsequent expressions of these ideas have been given on various other occasions.

A Christian View of Man

James Packer

Dr. James I. Packer was educated at Oxford University where he earned the D.Phil. in classics and theology. Ordained in 1952, he served as assistant minister at St. John's Church of England, Harborne, Birmingham. Later he became senior tutor at Tyndale Hall, an Anglican seminary in Bristol. Then, after nine years as warden of Latimer House, an Anglican evangelical study center in Oxford, he returned to Tyndale Hall as principal. When Tyndale Hall merged with two other colleges to become Trinity College, Bristol, he became associate principal. Currently, he is Professor of Systematic and Historical Theology, Regent College, Vancouver. Dr. Packer has preached and lectured widely and is a frequent contributor to theological periodicals. Among his books are *Fundamentalism and the Word of God*, *Evangelism and the Sovereignty of God*, *Knowing God*, *God Has Spoken*, *Knowing Man*, *Beyond the Battle for the Bible* and *God's Word*. He was an editor of the *New Bible Dictionary* and *The Bible Almanac*. With O. R. Johnston, he translated and edited Luther's *Bondage of the Will*.

In the days when theology was thought of as Queen of the Sciences, Christian concepts were treated as ultimate principles of explanation for everything—or maybe I should say, principles of ultimate explanation—since the claim was that though secondary causes operate throughout created reality, everything must be explained ultimately in terms of God, inasmuch as it exists ultimately by the will of God and not otherwise. At present, however, the Queen is exiled from most of the kingdoms of higher learning, and has been so for the best part of a hundred years, and palace revolutions have set secular world views and ideologies on her throne, to rule in her place. One result is that in those interdisciplinary discussions of life's great issues which every college and university worth its salt main-

101

tains, theologians often find themselves in the position of would-be immigrants denied entry at the border because their academic passports show them to be coming from the wrong quarter of the intellectual world. I wish therefore to begin by putting on record my delight that Hillsdale College, for one, keeps a place in its curriculum for Christian studies, and still allows that the Christian view of things might throw light into perplexing areas where, for lack of it, there is at present only ominous darkness.

Now let me tell you what I plan to do. My place in this series requires me to talk about man, and my role as a theologian commits me to talk about man in relation to God. That, however, tells you nothing about my method, and these are days in which you need to watch theologians like hawks because of the extraordinary madnesses of method in which as a fraternity we get enmeshed. So let me come clean about my own present purpose and procedure right away.

The array of intellectual enterprises which nowadays call themselves theology prove on inspection to be of two opposite sorts, each with its own set of mutations within the type as it interacts with the modern world. Some theologies start by taking from current culture fashionable hypotheses about the human race, hypotheses philosophical, physiological, psychological, anthropological, historical, and socio-economic; then, treating these as fixed points, they spend their strength editing and recasting the Christian tradition so as to make it fit these secular frames of reference. Other theologies take the Christian tradition itself as their frame of reference, within which they relativize, interpret and critique the secular hypotheses and the evidence on which they are based. Though the two-way traffic of mutual interrogation flows constantly between theologians of each camp, they cannot come very close to each other because their fixed points are so different. Those of type one usually label themselves liberal, those of type two conservative. Both groups are what they are because of what they believe to lie at the heart of the Christian tradition. Liberals find there noncognitive religious feelings or urges which for self-descriptive purposes clothe themselves in whatever verbal forms each culture may at any time provide; conservatives find there knowledge of facts about God and men which God himself has given by what he has told us or shown us. Alongside these two mutually exclusive approaches to the question of revelation (for that is what we are talking about here) there is no third option, though there are many confused and confusing compromises littering the theological scene. But every theologian — indeed, every Christian — does in fact come down on one side or other of this fence, even those who are sure they are sitting on it.

Now I am a theologian of the second type. I would rather call myself conservationist than conservative, lest I seem to embrace a closed-minded, change-resisting ideology as I fear my fundamentalist friends sometimes slip into doing. But I shall not fuss about words; you may call me a conservative, and I shall not complain! What I perceive at the heart of Christianity is God revealing himself in saving love by word and deed within mid-Eastern history, supremely in the incarnation whereby the second person of the Godhead walked and talked as a man among men, but also in the ministry of prophets and apostles and in the Scriptures which are the literary deposit of that ministry; and I perceive the historic Christian tradition, within which I stand and out of which I speak, as a sustained struggle to grasp and apply this uniquely given revelation. So I want to bring this revelation into the present, as best I can, for the light it throws on our perplexities about ourselves, and my hope, as you would expect, is to persuade you to embrace it as the guiding light for your life.

After that, it will not surprise you that I introduce what I have to say by an extract from the Bible. It comes in fact from the Old Testament, which Christians claim as Christian Scripture. We do that because Christ and his apostles, the founders of Christianity, did it before us. It is a Christian heresy to discount or drop the Old Testament, to which Christ appealed as the unchallengeable word of his Father which he had come to fulfill. Here, now, is the passage, Psalm 8, a song of praise to God for the way he has made man.

O Lord, our Lord,
   how majestic is your name in all
     the earth!

You have set your glory
   above the heavens.
From the lips of children and infants
   you have ordained praise
because of your enemies,
   to silence the foe and the avenger.

When I consider your heavens,
   the work of your fingers,
the moon and the stars,
   which you have set in place,
what is man that you are mindful of
     him,
   the son of man that you care for
     him?
You made him a little lower than the
     heavenly beings
   and crowned him with glory and
     honor.
You made him ruler over the works of
     your hands;
   you put everything under his feet:
all flocks and herds,
   and the beasts of the field,
the birds of the air,
   and the fish of the sea,
   all that swim the paths of the seas.

O Lord, our Lord,
   how majestic is your name in all
     the earth!

Well, what is man? I start my argument by picking up that
question as it relates to each human individual. It is an inescapable question which no one who thinks at all can avoid asking
about himself or herself. We find ourselves to be self-

transcendent, because we are self-conscious and self-aware. We can stand back from ourselves and look at ourselves and judge ourselves and ask basic questions about ourselves, and, what is more, we cannot help doing these things. The questions ask themselves, unbidden; willy-nilly, one finds oneself wondering what life means, what sense it makes, what one is here for. And such questions must be squarely faced.

Usually when we talk about man we are generalizing about mankind, and regularly we exempt ourselves from our own generalizations. We speak of the human race as if we were God looking down on it and not ourselves part of it. But that will not do. The acid test of our generalizations is whether we can apply them to ourselves, and live in terms of them as truths about ourselves. No generalizations about others which you are not prepared to apply to yourself have any claim to respectability, for you cannot contract out of the human race; and the moment you start applying them to yourself you abandon the impersonal, collectivist standpoint so beloved by human scientists, Western as well as Marxist, and come back to the problem of the individual—yourself—and the meaning of your own life.

Maybe you recall the scintillating speech in which Shakespeare's Hamlet says, "What a piece of work is man! how noble in reason! how infinite in faculty [*i.e.*, ability]! in form, in moving, how express and admirable! in action how like an angel! in apprehension how like a god! the beauty of the world! the paragon of animals!" Here Hamlet says brilliantly what Psalm 8 adumbrates and Christians have always said about man: namely, that he is a kind of cosmic amphibian. He has both a body and a mind and so has links with both apes and angels; he stands between animals who have no minds like his and angels who have no bodies like his. This is the classic Christian hierarchical view according to which the creatures are ranked in tiers, so to speak, below the Creator, at different levels of intrinsic complexity and significance in the cosmic order. Human beings are thus below angels but above the rest of the animate creation, over which mankind has actually been set to rule (Psalm 8:4–8, echoing Genesis 1:26–28). Each human individual, therefore, is wonderful, mysterious, resourceful, glorious.

But now, do you recall the plot of *Hamlet*? The quiveringly intelligent prince of Denmark is more than a mouthpiece for oracles; he is an individual in his own right, and an individual put on the spot, caught in a web of circumstances like a rat in a trap. Hamlet is charged by his father's ghost to take vengeance on the unspeakable Claudius; he cannot find a situation in which he can effectively do it, and ends as a victim of the malice that his efforts have aroused. That is the real plot of the play and the real agony of its hero, and it is this that makes *Hamlet* a tragedy in Aristotle's definitive sense—a pitiful, terrifying, cathartic story of destruction and waste, the waste of a good man and a potentially fruitful life, and the dragging down of others with him. Some tragedies (*Macbeth, Othello, King Lear* and most of Ibsen's plays, for instance) hinge upon a moral flaw or lapse which interacts with unfolding circumstances to bring about the protagonist's downfall. Other tragedies, however, like Sophocles' *King Oedipus*, Hardy's *Tess*, and *Hamlet*, work without this; they simply show us a noble person against whom the cards are stacked. The chilling fascination of their story then lies in the empathy we feel with the victim as the trap closes. For so much of life as we know it is like that!

And this brings us right back to the enigma of the individual, the problem of what it means to be me. Am I a hero, a victim, or just a nonentity in the world of which I am consciously part? How should I value myself? And how should I direct myself? How should I make decisions at such crunch points in life as the tragedies portray?

> "The play is the tragedy, 'Man',
> And its hero the conqueror Worm."

Is that all that can be said? Does life's ultimate frustration and waste consist in the fact that none of the things that seem important to us really mean anything? Is life, after all, a tale told by an idiot, full of sound and fury, signifying nothing? Is nobility, after all, a non-issue, as so many modern writers seem to think? Again I ask: what is man? For thinking people, as I said above, the question is inescapable.

More questions arise: the question of identity, for instance. Who are you? You don masks, you play roles; how, amid all that, can you identify, and identify with, the real you? Again, there is the question of goals. Has life a purpose? If so, which way should I go to fulfill it? That raises the question of destiny. What am I here for? What can I hope for? Intimations of immortality come to us all; the atheist resolutely squelches them; dare we trust them? If we do, we next must ask whether what we do now will affect what we experience then. In any case, we all have to die some day, and that brings up the question whether my future death will make nonsense of my life, as existentialists believe it will. Can I make sense of death? I think it was Dag Hammarskjöld who said that no philosophy which will not make sense of death is fit to be a guide for life, and surely he was right.

With all this comes the question of life's inner contradictions. Why do I so often feel lonely and unfulfilled and impotent and frustrated when I am doing things that I expected to enjoy? Take the matter of relationships. Life, we know, is essentially relationships, and the rich life is the life enriched by one's relationships. But how do enriching relationships happen? How are they achieved? And why do I seem to myself both to want them and not to want them? If close relationships are essential to my fulfillment, why do I shrink from them, as I seem to do? If however they are not essential to my fulfillment, why do I desire them, as again I seem to do? I am a human being in contradiction, a problem and a perplexity to myself. And aren't you the same?

Look at this quote:

Always I have seen around me all the games and parades of life and have always envied the players and the marchers. I watch the cards they play and feel in my belly the hollowness as the big drums go by, and I smile and shrug and say, Who needs games?

Who wants parades? The world seems to be masses of smiling
people who hug each other and sway back and forth in front of a
fire and sing old songs and laugh in each other's faces, all truth
and trust. And I kneel at the edge of the woods, too far off to
feel the heat of the fire. Everything seems to come to me in some
kind of secondhand way which I cannot describe. Am I not meat
and tears, bone and fears, just as they? Yet when most deeply
touched, I seem, too often, to respond with smirk or sneer,
another page in my immense catalog of remorses. I seem forever
on the edge of expressing the inexpressible, touching what has
never been touched, but I cannot reach through the veil of apart-
ness. I am living without being truly alive. I can love without
loving. When I am in the midst of friends, when there is laughter, closeness, empathy, warmth, sometimes I can look at myself
from a little way off and think that they do not really know who
is with them there, what strangeness is there beside them, trying
to be something else.

Once, just deep enough into the cup to be articulate about
subjective things, I tried to tell Meyer all this. I shall never forget
the strange expression on his face. 'But we are *all* like that!' he
said. 'That's the way it *is*. For everyone in the world. Didn't you
know?'

That soliloquy comes from John D. MacDonald's heroic
anti-hero Travis McGee, a modern Robin Hood with clay feet
whose James Bondish exploits in paperback may or may not
interest you. But I think you will agree that it pinpoints brilliantly this contradictory core of human experience, our recur-
ring sense of isolation within togetherness and of alienation
within community. " 'That's the way it *is*. For everyone in the
world. Didn't you know?' " But how should we account for this
universal state of affairs? Again we have to ask: what is man?

I am sure that, as members of the human race, you have been
with me in judgment and analysis thus far; I hope you will stay
with me as I proceed. For now I shall try to state the Christian
answer to some of these questions. Perhaps I had better be
more precise, and say: the *mainstream* Christian answer, as
given in the Bible and maintained in the church against eccen-

tric extremes ever since Christianity began. Essentially it is as follows. Every human individual has infinite worth, being made by God for nobility and glory; but every human individual is currently twisted out of moral shape in a way that only God can cure. To put it in standard Christian language, each of us by nature is God's image-bearer, but is also fallen and lives under the power of sin, and now needs grace. Sin, the anti-God allergy of the soul, is a sickness of the spirit, and the tragic sense of life, the inner tensions and contradictions just surveyed, plus our inveterate unrealism, egoism, and indisposition to love God and our neighbor, are all symptoms of our disorder. Sometimes Christians have expressed this thought by saying that man though good is terribly weak. That however seems hardly adequate, and I side with those who speak more strongly and say that each of us is radically bad, though providentially kept from expressing our badness fully. But in human nature, viewed morally, as God views it, everything is out of true to some extent. And though we have technology for straightening roads and integrating information, it is beyond us to straighten and integrate the human character. Man needs God for that.

This in a nutshell is the view I shall develop. But since a contrasting background makes things stand out more vividly, I shall before going further remind you of the main alternative views that are current in our culture. They each offer themselves in the name of humanism, a familiar word signifying the affirmation, celebration and attempted realization of human potential; from my standpoint, however, animalism would be a better name for them, since they all invite us to live as the lower animals do, without knowledge of or regard for the Creator— which in the theologically definitive sense of the word "human" is a sub-human state for a man to be in. Here, now, they are.

First comes *evolutionary optimism*, which is a secular version of the Christian heresy of self-salvation called Pelagianism. This is the view that our race and our world are actually and necessarily getting better as time goes by. This seems to me a forlorn idea which history and experience have comprehensively falsified; only a kind of faith that is impervious to facts can still maintain it. For half a century up to the second world war liberal church leaders in America backed and blessed the idea, thinking that the God of providence had committed himself to furthering the posited evolutionary process. But such talk is not heard from Christian thinkers today, and in an age when human survival is in question, evolutionary optimism must be judged to be just a form of whistling in the dark.

Second, and at the opposite extreme from optimistic unrealism, comes *existentialist pessimism*, which is a secular version of the Christian heresy of self-degradation called Manicheism. This latter-day oddity, whose prophets are men like Sartre and Camus, regards human life as intrinsically trivial and worthless. It sees Christian civilization, currently in decay (this, alas, can hardly be denied), as built on a belief in God and absolute moral values which is now exploded. It declares that life makes no sense, that man is in Sartre's phrase "a useless passion," and that the best formula for living is to be blindly wholehearted about something, for this at least keeps misery at bay and helps to pass the time! Though set forth with desperate seriousness, it is hard to treat this as a serious option.

(With it should be compared the far older *religious pessimism* of the Aryan East, embodied in Hinduism, Buddhism and their many variants, which during the past generation has spread widely in the English-speaking world. Here the basic idea is that by means of disciplined self-negation and asceticism one can escape the pains of retributive reincarnation through the dissolving away of one's separate personhood. Coping with suffering is the avowed agenda here, whereas coping with disillusionment is evidently the modern existentialist's concern.)

Third, and at the opposite extreme from individualistic pessimism, comes *manipulative determinism*, which is a secular version of the Christian belief in divine creation (new reaction) of individuals and societies. This ideology, as we ought to call it, whether in its Marxist-Leninist or in its Freudian-Skinnerian form, proposes by means of insistent propaganda and psychological conditioning (indoctrination and brainwashing) to make us into different and better people, and so produce a different and better society. In each case, of course, one group has to be excluded from the process, namely the manipulators themselves. Orwell imagined the result in his *1984*. Any who doubt whether infallibly wise philosopher-kings, such as Plato dreamed of, can actually be found to play the role of Big Brother, or who doubt the validity of the materialist and behaviorist assumptions on which this manipulative ideology rests, or who are old-fashioned enough to believe that God alone is lord of the conscience, will understandably be less than enthusiastic.

Against the background of these alternatives, I now proceed to elucidate the classic Christian answer to the question: what is man? I have four double-barreled points to develop, and the first thing to say is that for each of them Jesus of Nazareth, the Jesus of the four gospels, the perfect man who was God incarnate, is my center of reference. It cannot be said too strongly or too often that for Christians Jesus is both the model and the means of true and total humanness in a world where, as was said above, our own human nature has in every case been distorted and diminished by sin. Incarnation means that Jesus, who was one hundred percent divine, was also one hundred percent human, and it is supremely by observing his divine humanity that we learn what constitutes full and authentic humanness for ourselves. In Jesus we see what humanity is meant to be and what through Jesus' own mediation our flawed humanity may become. Now to my analysis.

The first point concerns the *dignity* and *dependence* of the individual.

Human dignity, yours and mine, and that of every human being without exception, flows from the fact that we are made in the image of God, as Genesis 1:26 and 5:1–2 affirm. What does that mean?, we ask. Clearly, the basic idea is that human beings are like God in a way that other animate creatures are not. How in detail to conceive this likeness is however a question that has exercised exegetes and theologians throughout the Christian era. The mainstream line of exposition is as follows. The *imago Dei* relationship relates not to our physical but to our personal nature, and this at four levels.

First, God, whom Genesis 1 and all Scripture presents as rational, made us rational, able to form concepts, think thoughts, carry through trains of reasoning, make and execute plans, live for goals, distinguish right from wrong and beautiful from ugly, and relate to other intelligent beings. This rationality is what makes us moral beings, and it is the basis for all other dimensions of Godlikeness, whether those given in our creation or those achieved through our redemption.

Second, God the Creator made us sub-creators under Him, able and needing to find fulfillment in the creativity of art, science, technology, construction, scholarship, and the bringing of order out of various sorts of chaos.

Third, God as Lord made us his stewards, that is, deputy managers—bailiffs, as the English say, or factors, to put it in Scotch—to have dominion over the estate which is his world. This role, which presupposes our rationality and creativity, is the special theme of Psalm 8. Man's unique privilege is to harness, develop and use the resources of God's world, not only making animate creatures and vegetation his food, but tapping the resources of raw materials and energy, in order to create culture for two ends which God has inseparably linked—his honor, and our joy. Such cultural activity is natural and instinctive to us.

Finally, God who Himself is good (truthful, faithful, wise, generous, loving, patient, just, valuing whatever has moral, intellectual or aesthetic worth and hating all that negates such worth) originally made man good in the sense of naturally and spontaneously righteous. Righteousness in man means active response to God by doing what He loves and commands and avoiding what he hates and forbids. God has a moral character, as you and I have, and there are specific types of action which he approves and others which he disapproves. Human nature as created has a teleological structure such that its fulfillment (which subjectively means our conscious contentment and joy) only occurs as we consciously do, and limit ourselves to doing, what we know that God approves. Unhappily, no one naturally lives this way; in terms of our Maker's design we all malfunction on the moral level, and need both His forgiveness and His inward renewing (new creation).

What Christians say about the image of God in mankind, therefore, with some variety of vocabulary but substantial unity· of sentiment, is that while we retain the image formally and structurally, and in terms of actual dominion over the created order, we have lost it materially and morally, and in terms of personal righteousness before our Creator.

Our dependence, which is the other half of my heading, has to do with our creaturehood. Because we depend on God for all good things, and indeed for our very existence moment by moment, we are obligated both to be grateful and to recognize ourselves as claimed by our Creator with absolute authority. The prevalent modern mood is certainly very different: in our fallenness and folly we crave independence of God as sovereign states crave independence of their neighbors — a syndrome which according to the Bible goes back to the Garden of Eden. But the result is enslavement to our own technology and skills, which instead of being our servants become our masters. The only way human beings can avoid bondage to things (objects, institutions, processes) and dreams (either of pleasure or of profit or of position) is by conscious subjection to the will of the living God "whose service is perfect freedom."

The Christian, giving his account of man, rests everything that he has to say on these basic facts of our dignity as God's image bearers and our dependence as His creatures; and he sees both this dignity and this dependence archetypically embodied and expressed in the life of Jesus Christ.

My second point concerns the *delight* and *development* of the individual: two more realities that belong together, as we shall see.

Christianity views mankind as made for delight, but by reason of our fallenness missing it. Joy is never the habitual experience of those who are not right with God: instead, they feel the pressure of the questions posed at the start of this paper, and this makes full and constant joy impossible. Shelley, himself an unbeliever, testified on behalf of all such when he said, "Rarely,

rarely comest thou, Spirit of delight." For God has sovereignly linked happiness with holiness and sin with misery, and to break these links is beyond our power. Only as life becomes love and worship of God, and love and service of our neighbor, in the knowledge of sins forgiven and heaven to come, does joy become unqualified and unending for us, as by Jesus' own testimony it was for him. But knowing God brings joy that grows, and this is the sort of development that matters most. And clearly, it is something which outward development in the form of increased wealth, skills, comfort, respect from others and range of choices cannot of itself guarantee.

The word *development* is most commonly used nowadays in an external sense and with a corporate reference-point. Thus, we speak of industrial, political and economic development of communities, and of the development of this or that communal enterprise. Mainstream Christianity in principle backs development of this kind, for it belongs to culture-building, which as was noted above is both our instinct and our appointed task. But mainstream Christianity has always attached more importance to the inward, individual development of persons in the way that brings delight even where outward deprivations perforce continue. That way is the way of spiritual development, the way of personal faith and practical godliness. While not refusing interest in external community development as Eastern religion has historically done, and while welcoming and indeed fostering such development, Christianity has always held that what matters most is the welfare of the individual in his or her relation to God. Thus, when William Booth's task force set out to bring the three S's (soup, soap, salvation) to the deprived poor, there was no question which was of first importance, and so they called themselves not the Soap or Soup Brigade but the Salvation Army.

It is true that a politicized, secularized version of Christianity, animated by an abstract egalitarianism, is abroad today, calling on churches to back rebellions and revolutions all 'round the world in the name of compassion for the poor. But this is, to say the least, eccentric by mainstream Christian standards. Historically, while calling for Samaritanship (the relief of others' needs) and aid for development (the creation of physical well-being), the church has for the most part remembered that nothing matters more than the spiritual welfare of individuals, and that its own first task is to spread the gospel, and that it must try to keep free of socio-economic and socio-political entanglements that would make this harder to do than it is already. Jesus Christ was poor, and most Christians to date have been poor too (it was not always and everywhere as it is in today's United States); but Jesus' delight in knowing, loving and serving the one whom he called Father did not depend on his becoming part of any process of community development, nor has the joy of any Christian heart ever sprung from such a source. In an era like ours which idolizes material development this needs to be underlined.

The point can be sharpened if we focus for a moment on the question of freedom. The world assumes that the essence of freedom is to be free *from* this or that external pressure: poverty, race prejudice, economic exploitation, political injustice and the like. But that is only freedom's outward shell; it is not the real thing. The essence of true freedom is being free *for* what matters most — free, that is, for God and godliness, and so for the delight which grace and godliness together bring. The only way into that freedom, however, is to be set free from the egocentricity which binds us by nature, and that is something which Jesus Christ himself alone can do. Which leads to my final points.

Third, I want to add to what I have already said about the *design* and *deformity* of the individual.

Christianity sees each person as designed for a life beyond this life — an endless life which for those who know God will be far richer and more joyous than our present life can be, and for which life in this world was always meant to be a preparation. The Christian valuation of personal spiritual welfare as more important than any socio-economic benefit depends ultimately on the knowledge that this world passes away, while the world to come is eternal. We were never intended to treat this world as home, or live in it as if we would be here forever; Jesus pictured the man who lives that way as a fool. But, whether or not it is true, as is often affirmed (though I am not convinced), that belief in heaven may discourage Christians from doing all the good they can on earth, it is beyond doubt that mockery from Marxists and other skeptics at the idea of "pie in the sky, by and by, when you die" has made today's Western church feel embarrassed at having a hope of heaven, fearing lest it be howled at as a cop-out from social responsibility; so in fact very little gets spoken about that hope at the present time. (It was different, be it said, in Uganda under the Moslem butcher Amin, and in Kenya in the Mau Mau days, just as it was for the first three Christian centuries, during which time Christianity was officially outlawed and any believers might find themselves facing lions in the arena at any time.) Yet it is the way of human nature as God designed it to live in and by one's hopes, and part of the real Christian's joy, increasing with age, is to look forward to eternal life in resurrection glory with the Father and the Son. Christians have sometimes described this present life, first to last, as preparation for dying, which might sound to modern ears like a gruesome and neurotic fancy; but in light of God's design of us as hoping animals the statement is really no more than a matter-of-fact indication of the truly natural outlook for us all.

But the children of our secular, materialistic culture decline to live, even to think of living, in terms of the world to come, and this, along with actual irreligion and egocentric immorality, constitutes the inward deformity which Christianity sees in fallen human beings. However handsome the face and however beautiful the body, the soul—that is, the real person—is out of shape and ugly. This deformity leads to a constant diffused discontent with things as they are, a miserable old age (because one has less and less to look forward to) and, one fears, a yet more miserable eternity. The Christian vision of each unregenerate person is accordingly of a tragic ruin—a noble creation originally, but one now spoiled and wasted, and tragically so by reason of the great potential for good and for joy that has thus been lost.

This shows why thoughtful Christians have always seen missionary ministry as the church's top priority in this world. Since it is only as individuals become Christians that the ruins of their lives get rebuilt, evangelism is service of each person's deepest need, and is thus the truest love of one's neighbor. The compassion that drives Christians at this point was verbalized thus in Old Testament times:

> Come, all you who are thirsty, come to the waters; and you who have no money, come, buy and eat! Come, buy wine and milk without money and without cost. Why spend money on what is not bread, and your labor on what does not satisfy? Listen, listen to me, and eat what is good, and your soul will delight in the richest of fare. . . . Seek the Lord while he may be found; call on him while he is near. Let the wicked forsake his way and the evil man his thoughts. Let him turn to the Lord, and he will have mercy on him, and to our God, for he will freely pardon (Isaiah 55:1-2, 6-7).

Fourth, I want to say a little more about the *delivering* and *deprogramming* of the individual who is found by God's grace.

The heart of the Christian message is that the Christ who exhibited in Himself true and full humanness according to the Creator's intention, and who diagnosed the spiritual deformity that sin brings, and the personal disasters to which it leads, more trenchantly than was ever done before or since, died sacrificially to redeem us from sin; rose triumphantly from death; and now lives to forgive and remake us, and turn us by His power from the travesties of humanity that we really are into authentic human beings who bear His moral image. By His death and the forgiveness that flows from it He delivers us from God's condemnation; by leading us through His word in Scripture into the paths of discipleship, and by the transforming work of His Spirit at the level of our instincts, inclinations, insights and attitudes (what Scripture calls our *heart*), He deprograms us from the game plans of our former ungodly self-centeredness, teaching us to look at everything through His eyes and literally to live a new life. His word to the world is still: "Come to me, all you who are weary and burdened, and I will give you rest. Take my yoke upon you and learn from me . . . and you will find rest for your souls" (Matthew 11:28–29). Through Scripture and the Spirit He still fulfills this promise. In this sense Christianity is, and always will be—Christ himself.

Whether you who read these words will believe them and turn to Christ accordingly is something that I cannot arrange on your behalf, much as I wish I could. But at least I can require you to take proper note of the fact that this, and nothing less than this, is the message of biblical and historic mainstream Christianity. The widespread idea that Christianity celebrates the value of the individual by affirming his natural goodness and then teaching him how to do even better is false. Christianity diagnoses the individual as morally distorted and spiritually ruined, as we saw, and against that dark background points to Christ as the only one who can straighten out our twisted natures. That task is like re-railing a derailed train; passengers pushing will not suffice to get it back on the track; a crane must do what is beyond the power of human muscle. I am saying that Jesus Christ remakes us in his own moral and spiritual image, and that this is something which we cannot do for ourselves by our own resources. I am further saying, therefore, that at some point along the line each of us must come to the point of admitting that we need to be saved, since we cannot save ourselves. We have not got what it takes to re-order our disordered lives; we need to be saved by Jesus Christ. It is those who in humble honesty reach that moment of truth who become Christians.

And this, so I urge, is the true humanism, the true formula for human fulfillment. It is a humanism which has the Creator at its center and, as I said before, Christ as its model and means. It is the true freedom, freedom for God and goodness, which is only found under authority—the personal, unqualified authority of the living Christ. It is the freedom which Solzhenitsyn found in the Gulag where, stripped of all he had and of all his dignity in human terms, he put his faith in Jesus Christ. It is, to be sure, a life of compassion and distress; looking through Christian eyes at the way in which your fellow men ruin their lives, and involve others again and again in their own disasters, will drive you to tears. Your understanding of the nature, value and needs of individuals will make much in our society abhorrent to you—the disrespect for God-given life, and for God its giver, that is involved in abortion on demand and in the advocacy of euthanasia and suicide, for instance; plus the frivolity of so many towards marriage vows, the cruelty of so many towards parents, spouses and children, our indifference to the needs of lonely elderly folk, the inhumaneness of our prison system, and a great deal more. The Christian will be for justice, but as he will not equate this with egalitarianism so he will not regard callousness towards those who offend both him and society at large as part of what justice requires. Perhaps the most authentic expression of Christian humanism will be the devotion which the believer, following his Master, will show to meeting the needs of his fellow men as they confront him. He will not be passive. He will be like the Samaritan in Jesus' parable, seeing others as comparable to the beaten-up Jew in the gutter and seeing himself as obliged to stop and help. Most of all will he try to help them, with all other forms of help that he offers, to listen to God, to take note of Jesus Christ, and to find their way into a living relationship with him, for he knows that their spiritual need is their greatest need of all. And in doing so he will be endlessly hopeful, for he knows that he works with God.

Such, then, in outline is the Christian view of man, and the root principles of the humanism that is based on it. As I close I feel bound to express my conviction that the health of Western society is directly bound up with a return to it; not only do I see it as a constructive alternative, but the dominant secular view of man, the creation of the Enlightenment, of Darwin and of Freud, whether in its optimistic, pessimistic, or deterministic mold, appears to me to be utterly bankrupt, with its insolvency showing more clearly every year. Therefore I hope with all my heart that in our time the Christian vision of godly humanness will catch hold of the Western imagination once more. I hope you may share that hope with me.

Christian Studies and Liberal Arts: Are They Compatible?

Thomas J. Burke

Dr. Thomas J. Burke is presently a faculty member of Hillsdale College with teaching specialties in the philosophy of religion, historical theology, epistemology, and biblical studies. He earlier taught at the Sacred Heart School of Theology, Hales Corner, Wisconsin. Burke received his bachelor of arts degree from Baylor University and went on to earn the M.Div. from Trinity Evangelical Divinity School and his Ph.D. from Northwestern University. Dr. Burke has also earned a master's in philosophy from Michigan State University where he is in the final stages of completing his second doctorate. Burke's research into the relationship between science and religion has resulted in a study published recently by the *Journal of the American Scientific Affiliation* entitled, "The Mind-Body Problem: Scientific or Philosophic?"

In the not-too-distant past, to question the compatibility of Christian studies with the liberal arts would have been unthinkable. The liberal arts were considered part and parcel of a total educational system not only permeated with Judeo-Christian concepts and values, but also culminating in a theological view of life and the world which saw Christian theism as the intellectual as well as the spiritual crown of learning. The liberal arts had their own purpose and did not exist merely as a propaedeutic for theology, but they were a necessary preparation for theology on the one hand and were not in themselves considered adequate for a comprehensive and complete view of the world on the other. Moreover, they depended on Christian truths for their own proper development. Indeed, a fundamental knowledge of the Bible and basic Christian ideas about God and the world were presupposed in the liberal arts curriculum.

121

How, indeed, it was felt, could one study ethics without some knowledge of what Jesus said about one's treatment of his fellow human being? How could there be any proper metaphysical understanding of reality without knowing that the world was created by an eternal and omnipotent God? How could one have a proper and accurate view of history if he was ignorant of or disregarded the most vital and earth-shaking occurrence in history, the central determinative event in the saga of mankind, equalled in importance only by the creation itself, namely, the incarnation of the Son of God in Jesus of Nazareth and the matrix of salvific acts which He accomplished, culminating, of course, in his resurrection from the dead and his enthronement at the right hand of God? How could one have any objective view of the nature and function of human life if he did not consider history and human existence in the context of the future climax of history at the return of that same Jesus?

A proper education was not possible outside the framework of Christian beliefs because those beliefs were held to be well-attested, objective facts that anyone who really wanted a truthful knowledge of human existence could not possibly ignore without greatly distorting his perception, not to say his conception, of the world. The role of the liberal arts was to help one understand, explicate, appreciate, and apply that Christian world view, to flesh it out, so to speak, with a knowledge of history, literature, art, and the sciences so that the Christian man might also be a cultured and knowledgeable person. Such a vision of the role of liberal arts, however remote it may seem to us, was the underlying view which motivated the founding of institutions such as Oxford, Cambridge, Harvard, Yale, and Princeton. To one raised in that understanding of the liberal arts, the question before us would appear absurd.

Today, the very mention of a Christian Studies Program immediately raises questions of academic integrity and compatibility with the presumed objectivity and critical understanding of the liberal arts. Something has changed. That something is actually a very complex historical development which includes not only the secularization of the liberal arts, *i.e.*, the gradual acceptance of the belief that each discipline can function independently of any other and, specifically, independently of any religious ideas, but also a growing skepticism regarding the basic beliefs of Christian theism which made them seem optional. In addition, however, Christian theology itself became severely skeptical towards its own objectivity and truth. Non-cognitive conceptions of theological knowledge became the standard within as well as without theological circles, and faith and reason were juxtaposed in such a way that religion was robbed of any possible basis for claiming the sort of knowledge appropriate for a college liberal arts curriculum. Religion, it was felt, was a matter of private belief and functioned on the emotive, subjective level. The only place it had in academia, then, was as the object of study from an historical perspective or as the subject of philosophical, sociological and psychological analysis. The actual beliefs themselves were considered outside the realm of objectivity. One could study them, but ought not incorporate them into the interpretation of existence incumbent upon academia to inculcate. Ironically, of course, one could teach professedly non-cognitive philosophies of life such as existentialism, but that is another story.

Significantly, all the major schools of thought in this century, existentialism, logical positivism, humanism, and even theology itself were agreed that religion was non-cognitive, that the basis for religious belief was unobservable, subjective experience, and that the events claimed as support for Christian theism were either fabricated or true only in *Heilsgeschichte* and observable only to the eyes of faith. *Ipso facto*, noting the exceptions mentioned above, religion, particularly Christian theism, was felt to be incompatible with the professedly rational and factually oriented liberal arts, and most certainly, its fundamental tenets ought not be included in any contributory manner in a liberal arts curriculum.

Three fundamental shifts in our perspective of religion, it appears, lie at the heart of our immediately skeptical reaction towards a Christian Studies Program. First, the view that religion is non-cognitive. Second, the belief that there are no good reasons to accept the fundamental tenets of the Christian religion and, conversely, the conviction that adherence to them arises only out of blind faith. Third, the idea that either metaphysical beliefs are at best unnecessary and at worst meaningless or, if legitimate, must be restricted to those that can be founded on philosophical reason alone. Religious ideas, being non-cognitive, it was said, have no place in an academic environment.

Given this outlook, what then does a liberal arts curriculum attempt to accomplish today? An explication of the liberal arts from a contemporary perspective will include the following: First, the liberal arts will attempt to introduce students to their heritage. They should impart a knowledge of the great ideas which have been instrumental in the development of our culture and the understanding we have of our world, and make familiar the significant events, persons and achievements which have been instrumental in our history. Second, a liberal arts education will develop within students the ability to engage in critical and rational thought, to evaluate and adopt those ideas and beliefs they find valuable because well supported by good arguments and to reject those they find unsupported. Third, it will supply students with the tools necessary to develop their own world view, their own set of values and beliefs about what is and how it is, and to critically evaluate both their own ideas and those of others. Fourth, a liberal arts education will aim at developing an appreciation for that art, music, theatre, literature, etc. which is worthy of appreciation. Fifth, a liberal arts education should help form students' characters in terms of honesty, integrity, and the other moral values upon which any civilization is built. In short, a liberal arts education will attempt to develop understanding, insight and both analytic and synthetic skills in order to create a well-informed, critically aware human being who is self-consciously rational and moral.

Given this conception of the liberal arts and a liberal arts education, does a Christian Studies Program or Christianity itself any longer have a place on the campus of a liberal arts college worthy of the name? The remainder of this paper shall argue that, indeed, a Christian Studies Program has not only a rightful, but a necessary place on any campus professing a commitment to objectivity, liberality, and culture. We shall first elaborate the nature and purpose of Hillsdale's Christian Studies Program. Second, we shall evaluate the most obvious objections to such an endeavor and show that they are founded upon either irrational prejudices or uninformed opinions. Finally, we shall argue that Christianity provides a framework which is at least, if not significantly more, compatible with the pursuance of a liberal arts education than any of its present alternatives.

I

The first task facing anyone attempting to explicate and defend the establishment of a Christian Studies Program on the campus of a non-church-affiliated liberal arts college is that of defining as precisely as possible what the intended program purports to be and to accomplish. There is, however, a preliminary question that must be addressed, namely, why a Christian Studies Program, and not, say, a Hindu or Moslem Studies Program? Although founded by Free-Will Baptists in 1844, Hillsdale College no longer has any affiliation with a religious body. Its student population is a microcosm of the society of which it is a part. Students attend Hillsdale from a variety of religious backgrounds and many have no interest in any religion whatsoever. Freedom of religion on the campus of Hillsdale College means virtually the same as it does in any of the fifty states and the District of Columbia, freedom to believe in and practice any religion one wishes, regardless of how bizarre, ill-founded, superstitious, or ridiculous, or, if one wishes, to neglect, avoid, spurn, or harangue any and all concourse with the gods and goddesses proffered by the purveyors of sanctity and priestly ministrations. Why, then, a Christian Studies Program?

The answer is fundamentally historical. No liberal arts education worth its *summa cum laude* can offer a truly adequate education unless it makes an effort to offer a comprehensive and accurate understanding of that religion which has provided the foundation and the intellectual context of our civilization for the past 1,500 years. If one of the purposes of a liberal arts education is to pass on a knowledge and appreciation of one's heritage, it would simply be inappropriate to leave out those beliefs and practices which a majority of those who created that heritage considered the most important part of their lives and the inspiration, both emotional and intellectual, for their thought and labors. There do indeed exist other great religious traditions with similar influences upon their cultures and civilizations, and for their universities and colleges to neglect them would be most inappropriate. Indeed, for us to totally neglect them would be a significant failure. But in trying to understand the world in which we live, it is imperative that we correctly evaluate the world from which we have come.

Moreover, Christianity has not existed in isolation from the intellectual mainstream. It has been interwoven into the very fabric of the Western mind, and not only priests and and prelates have thought they were doing God's bidding, but philosophers, scientists, poets, and artists have pursued their life's calling—or for some, compulsion—because they considered themselves the instruments of divine providence and engaged in an essentially spiritual task. Trying to plumb the thought of Dante, Chaucer, Shakespeare, Milton, Donne, or Hawthorne without an understanding of the theology which formed not only the background, but the focus of their conception of reality (although such exegesis is actually miraculously practiced), is to inevitably give rise to twisted and misshapen views of their ideas. In science Newton considered himself a theologian, Kepler sought God's mind through an examination of His creation, and the list could be extended endlessly. But the point is merely that the intellectual history of Western man is imbued with the contours, colors, and hues of the Christian conception of God and the world.

This historical fact alone is sufficient justification for a program that would aim to exposit the fundamental beliefs of

Christianity and bring to that exposition a modicum of objectivity. The continued shabby misrepresentation and ignoring of the content and formative influence of Christian theology will only give rise to generations of scholars who can but misunderstand, misinterpret and misinform. A program is needed that will fill the theological void which characterizes most students entering college and give them a *sine qua non* for a well-rounded and accurate view of Western culture.

Christianity, however, is not a monolithic structure. The problem of limits must be faced not only vis-à-vis non-Christian points of view, but also in regard to the options available within Christianity itself. Again, the past provides the rule. It is Christianity in general, Christianity as it has existed in its main and minor streams throughout the past 2,000 years, a Christianity roughly sketched by C. S. Lewis in *Mere Christianity*, which has had the formative impact on Western culture. It encompasses both Roman Catholic and Protestant forms, for these have provided the main frameworks in which Western man has created his world view. Both these traditions of Western Christianity have in common belief in an Infinite, Spiritual, Perfect, Personal and Triune God as Creator, Preserver, and Redeemer of mankind. Moreover, both believe God has brought salvation to man through the incarnation, death, and resurrection of his only-begotten Son, Jesus Christ. Both see man as fallen from grace and in desperate need of forgiveness of sins and reunion with God. While it is most certainly necessary to examine the differences which exist among the varying groups of Christians and the different cultures which have arisen therefrom, the program itself makes no attempt to arbitrate among them, to declare some truly Christian and others not. Consequently, Hillsdale's Christian Studies Program is in the first place nonsectarian.

In the second place, the Christian Studies Program is interdisciplinary. It includes not only the study of Christian theology, but the expression of the Christian world view as it has been expressed in literature, philosophy, the arts, and in its historical and economic connections. Christianity presents not merely a religious picture of the religious sector of life; it also encompasses a metaphysical vision of reality and a comprehensive set of values which touch every aspect of human existence. It is a total world view, and hence can only be fully appreciated and understood if explored in all its manifestations. To accomplish this, all the various disciplines of the liberal arts must be employed.

Thirdly, it is integrative. The Christian Studies Program attempts not merely to give students a smattering of Christian glosses over miscellaneous topics, a sort of preacher's tour of the flora and fauna of the liberal arts, but also to allow them to explore the many-faceted nature of the Christian vision of the world, to see the implications of that vision for various areas of human life, and to understand the relations which this vision establishes between itself and the subjects comprising the liberal arts.

The first aim of this non-denominational, interdisciplinary, and integrative program is to develop an adequate knowledge of Christian theology and an accurate comprehension of how that theology has impinged upon the history and culture of Western civilization. The average student today knows little if anything of the theology of Christianity. Most of what is thought to be Christian doctrine actually has little to do with what Christianity has taught historically. Courses on specific subject matters cannot hope to cover those subjects and supply an adequate understanding of the rich and variegated theology which formed the world view of the men and times being studied. An invaluable preparation would be a program which would supply a thorough and comprehensive overview of Christian thought, exposing students to the drama of the biblical episodes and personalia which form the foundation of the Christian vision, expounding and examining the theological concepts of revelation, creation, and redemption which form the intellectual framework for that point of view, and exploring the idea of society and personal human conduct which the people of the past envisioned as normative. Given the historical development of our culture, such an aim can hardly be gainsaid. It is no different than any other course of study, except that it is directed toward the exposition and exploration of Christianity and the ways in which it has helped shape Western man and his civilization. Certainly, a school whose stated aim is to inculcate "traditional Western values" ought to have a place in its curriculum for such a program.

The second purpose of the Christian Studies Program, however, is not quite so easily appreciated. The program also aims at providing participants with a view of our history and culture from the perspective of Christian faith and an opportunity to think about our present situation from that intellectual and moral viewpoint. In other words, it aims not only at expositing Christianity, but also at promoting it as a viable intellectual, ideational, and moral world view.

II

Once such a purpose is expressed, a horde of seemingly sane objections to such an endeavor rushes to the surface. At the core of these objections are the problems of objectivity and freedom of thought, and I shall try to demonstrate that in this regard Christianity is no worse off than any other philosophical world view. The problems of objectivity and freedom will be dealt with under the topics of rationality and the revisability of beliefs, and I will attempt to show that objections in terms of these concepts are neither warranted nor insurmountable.

First, does not such an avowed objective run counter to the very essence of a liberal arts education? Is not a fundamental purpose of a liberal arts education to teach students to think for themselves, to think critically and objectively? Does not this radical objectivity demand the examination of ideas bounded by the limits of reason and evidence alone? How can such an examination occur when it begins from a perspective with an avowedly predetermined set of ideas on foundational issues?

In reply, it must first be noted that the goal of objective, critical thought is no more ruled out by a Christian Studies

Program than by any other approach to the subject matter of the arts. Why is a Christian Studies Program inimical to critical thinking while an investigation of the same subject areas from the perspective of atheism, humanism, or Marxism is not? Since the foremost universities in the world have avowed exponents of those viewpoints presenting their perspective on subjects within the liberal arts, how is it that they are compatible with a liberal arts education and Christianity is not? Once these questions are asked, it becomes evident that this objection is based on a fundamental misunderstanding of Christianity on the one hand and of the actual procedure of classroom instruction in a liberal arts education on the other.

It is sometimes supposed that in an academic university professors present to their students pure facts, reality as it exists when perceived objectively. Interpretations of those facts which are given in class are those which an anonymous, unprejudiced reason has demanded. The professor, it is assumed, stands above the partisan prejudices of parties and powers, and students simply inhale and distill the facts as presented and develop for themselves the most rational interpretation of the subject available.

Such is the theory, but hardly, given the realities of human rational and epistemic limitations, the truth. Facts are indeed doled out, but in the context of a particular understanding of their meaning and their relation to other "facts." Alternative positions are examined and arguments against them given, and, in turn, arguments for the position being presented are proposed and defended. After all, how does one think all those little logical positivists were propagated in the thirties, forties and fifties? By a purely objective display of the epistemological and linguistic facts of life? That would hardly account for the fact that such creatures are today an archaic rarity. They were consciously conceived, nurtured, and birthed in the classroom by instructors who would have shouted foul had a Christian or a Jew argued as prejudicially for the validity of his own position.

Please do not misunderstand. I am not saying the logical positivist should not have so taught his classes. Convinced of the righteousness of his cause, he could and should not have approached the subject in any other way. But if such a procedure is allowable for such an obviously inadequate metaphysical position, then surely the much more coherent, encompassing and ethically sophisticated position of Christianity ought to be given the same liberty.

Despite the limitations of the educational procedure, like democracy, it is the best of all known alternatives. Students are no more the mere gullible pawns of their professors than they are the mere image of their parents. Eventually, some do see the shortcomings, fallacies, and limitations of what they have been taught and seek out new viewpoints that will offer a more adequate solution to perennial intellectual quandaries. But there are certain metaphysical limits within which one must construct his interpretations of and theories about the world. One either is or is not a theist, and the interpretations, theories, etc. which one forms will necessarily be constrained by the position he or she takes on that issue. There is no high and holy ground of unadulterated objectivity from which a person can adjudicate by reason alone what is and what is not true.

One might respond that this is all well and good, but as a matter of fact, Christianity requires, on the basis of faith alone, belief in things that cannot be rationally proven and that contradict rational and critical thinking while other positions do not. In reply, it should first be noted that the assertion that Christianity requires certain things be accepted on faith alone without proof or evidence is simply incorrect. One may or may not find the evidence and arguments for Christian faith satisfactory, but that Christians have argued by a host of apologetic procedures for the basic, fundamental convictions of their ideas is evident from the long history of Christian apologetics, natural theology and historical and biblical investigations into the source and support of those ideas; endeavors, by the way, that continue vigorously on the contemporary scene. Even those theologians who have argued that it is impossible to reason someone into the faith have given reasons why this is so, and have through those arguments attempted to give reasons why a "leap of faith" should be made.

But such an apologetic approach is not, historically, the dominant one, and the mainstream of Christian apologetics has been constructed on the assumption that it was possible to show that such belief is warranted by the evidence. St. Augustine, for example, whose statement that unless he believed he could not understand has been the cause of much misapprehension of his epistemological position, was not proffering fideism; his personal trek towards faith was accomplished with the most intense reasoning and arduous mental efforts. He struggled with metaphysical, spiritual, and empirical data which led him to the intellectual conclusion that only Christianity, of all the intellectual options of the day, could satisfactorily account for the world as he knew it. Even after professing belief in Christ, he manfully sought to show why the skepticism of the Academy was wrong, not merely from the perspective of faith, but on the quite explicitly rational grounds that it failed to do justice to man's experience of his world and was woefully inadequate both intellectually and pragmatically. In other words, while taking as his starting place the presuppositions of Christian faith, he also felt it possible to establish the superiority of those presuppositions to any other set. Pascal, often cited as the fideist *par excellence*, by no means believed that one must simply leap to belief with no more than the pragmatic motivation that one was thereby making the best bet possible. He felt the historical evidences for the truth of Christianity were sufficient to warrant belief. Fideism, with the possible exception of Kierkegaard, is primarily a twentieth-century phenomenon propagated by those who have essentially abandoned the faith expressed in Scripture and creed as historically understood.

Secondly, in reply to the objection that Christianity demands the irrational acceptance of certain beliefs, it should be stressed that no one comes to any subject matter devoid of basic fundamental presuppositions. The atheist, agnostic, humanist—secular or religious—all have their own metaphysical baggage, and that baggage is as evident in their critiques of various positions as are the Christians'. Just as there exist no deductively conclusive arguments for the God of Christian theism, so there exist no deductively valid disproofs of his existence. Yet an unbeliever will insist that his objections make faith an intellectual impossibility, while upon listening intently and sympathetically to those objections, the Christian is stunned by the fact that such pitifully unsatisfactory and faulty arguments can so confidently persuade so intelligent a person. What seems like impeccable logic to the unbeliever, seems woefully inadequate to the believer. Likewise, I am sure, the non-Christian feels similarly when the Christian gives his reasons for his convictions.

As an example of this phenomenon, let me cite a philosopher friend of mine who insists that the problem of evil makes theism an intellectual impossibility. He feels the difficulties involved in harmonizing the existence of an omnipotent and omnibenevolent God with the existence of evil are so severe that the existence of the former is unthinkable. When it is pointed out that no logical contradiction exists and that, therefore, God's existence cannot be ruled out *a priori*, one is met with arguments of "probability" and "improbability." But such appeals are inapplicable to single-case situations, of which the existence of God is surely one; a fact pointedly and repeatedly made by non-theists when theists, in the absence of deductive proof, appeal to such probability. But one cannot have it both ways. If probability is inapplicable to and, therefore, logically unsupportive of theistic arguments, it is just as inapplicable to and logically unsupportive of atheistic arguments.

But what causes this almost innate reaction on both sides to arguments for the other position and against one's own? Primarily the fact that certain metaphysical views are held sacrosanct by the one and not the other. And make no mistake, at the bottom are metaphysical presuppositions, not purely rational principles, employed by the one and ignored by the other. When Martin Luther lashed out at "reason, the great whore," he was not asserting that in theology one could expostulate free of any constraints of logical consistency or reasonable support, that blind faith and heteronomous authority should supply the parameters and guidelines of theological thinking. He was rebelling against the bilious disgorgings of a reason bloated with fatuous ideas and assumptions which kept men from reading accurately the authoritative divine revelation in the Bible and seeing exactly what it was God was saying to man.

The "reason" to which modern-day rationalism, naturalism, and humanism appeal, like the Enlightenment "reason" before them, is neither the "empty," and necessarily universally accepted, principles of logic nor the logical priority of data over theory, but includes definite convictions concerning the nature of man, the nature of knowledge, and the metaphysical constitution of ultimate reality which are as unsupported by either evidence or logic as anything asserted by theists. Without metaphysics, rationality is bankrupt, indeed, impossible. It is those bedrock principles which supply the basis for "rational" critique; without them we are left to an insipid pragmatism which, of course, is a position which has, in the final analysis, given up on rationality and cannot, therefore, cast accusations of irrationality at Christianity.

This is not meant to imply that each one simply follows the predetermined course of his metaphysical presuppositions. Those presuppositions are debatable, individually and collectively, and the fact of "conversion" to and from various outlooks shows that we are not simply the pawns of our prior assumptions. It is important to realize, however, that pure objectivity is impossible, even to God, for surely His evaluation of the world is in terms of His basic beliefs. Hopefully, of course, He is and knows He is right while we merely think we might be. Pure rationality, deductive or inductive, is a myth that does not stand up under critical examination of the facts.

The second major criticism that might be leveled against a Christian Studies Program is that Christianity is a dogmatic position and, therefore, self-criticism and the revisability of theories is excluded by its exclusivistic claims. That, however, is simply not the case. Certainly, a church seminary ought to defend, not attempt to subvert, the basic tenets of the church which supports it. But a Christian Studies Program is not bound by the same strictures. It ought to be free to give the same critical evaluation of its own position as it gives of others.

In fact, openness to new ideas, to change and development in its concepts and theories, is written into the very presuppositions of Christianity. The Christian faith presupposes a God of truth, the real existence of a physical world, and a God-given ability on the part of human beings to know truth. Since truth is, accordingly, objective and discernable through the investigation of physical reality, there exists not only real purpose in investigating that world, but also a firm basis for confidence that such exploration will yield belief-worthy results. It is no accident that scientific method arose only on the soil of a civilization permeated with Christian metaphysical presuppositions, for those assumptions are essential if one is to view the world as amenable to scientific study and if one is to have confidence that such investigation will produce valuable results. Not even the Greeks with their penetrating analytic minds were able to develop a truly scientific method of research. The historian Herbert Butterfield writes, "It was not until Aristotelian physics had been overthrown in other regions altogether that the [Copernican] hypothesis could make any serious headway, . . . even in modern times."[1] As brilliant as he was, Aristotle could not advance beyond an observational knowledge of the world because he lacked the essential intellectual ingredients necessary for a truly scientific procedure. To mention just one, Stanley Jaki, states in his "Gifford Lectures," "The Aristotelian universe was necessary and so was its form of intelligibility, but this intelligibility served no real purpose, just as its universe had none, although it seemed to teem with purpose."[2] In other words, since the universe was seen as simply the necessary development and expression of rational ideas and unchangeable essences, even given the possibility of science, there was no real purpose in pursuing it.

More importantly, the missing ingredient for the development of science was Christian theism. As Jaki states later in the same work,

---

[1]Herbert Butterfield, *The Origins of Modern Science* (New York: The Free Press, 1965), p. 45.
[2]Stanley L. Jaki, *The Road of Science and The Ways to God* (Chicago: The University of Chicago Press, 1978), p. 25.

> Yet, as it turned out, the rise of science needed the broad and persistent sharing by the whole population, that is, an entire culture, of a very specific body of doctrines relating the universe to a universal and absolute intelligibility embodied in the tenet about a personal God, the Creator of all.[3]

The misreading of the history of science by White[4] and others has made it appear that it was blind adherence to an archaic bible and irrational dogma that was science's worst enemy. Of course, the Bible was quoted in defense of a Ptolemaic universe, but with no more justification than its use by advocates of slavery in the 1850s. The usage of the Bible in both instances makes it clear that it was employed as a tool for religious rationalization of previously held scientific and moral — or perhaps I should say pseudo-scientific and immoral — views. Certainly, both the Bible and dogma can be misused, but that is by no means a legitimate criticism of their own validity.

Confirmation that theological foundations are necessary for the development and appreciation of science can be seen in the gradual growth of mistrust in science and the mytho-poetical views of its nature which have arisen along with the decline in acceptance of those fundamental theological convictions largely responsible for its origin. Instrumentalist and pragmatic views of science abound, scientists are painted as artists merely fashioning the universe in their own image, science is reduced to a sort of intellectual white cane by which human beings are enabled to feel their way through the universe, and the basic rationale for endeavoring in such an effort is held to lie in the technical advances which make life easier for men. Gone, or at least rapidly dwindling, are the moral and spiritual values which alone can adequately sustain the arduous and often frustrating endeavor of scientific investigation, and gone with them are the basic theological convictions about the world and God which supply the undergirding ontological and epistemic support for

---

[3]*Ibid.*, p. 33.
[4]A. D. White, *A History of the Warfare of Science with Theology* (London, 1896).

reasonable confidence in science as a way to truth. Given the groundwork of Christian theism, science can be seen as the most efficient and epistemologically sound method of gaining truth about the world; without them, it is at best a handy tool by which man can satisfy his native intellectual curiosity and alleviate his physical and psychological needs.

Now, if Christian theology has and can supply the metaphysical foundations of that method of investigation most certain to supply us in the long run with true knowledge about the world, then it cannot at the same time be an irrational and dogmatic obstruction to truth. Certainly, there might be a reticence on the part of individual Christians to ideas and concepts which clash, or seem to clash, with long-cherished convictions. But that is no more true of Christians than naturalists, humanists, and Marxists. Indeed, I would argue that the former are more open to scientific truth than any of the latter. For example, committed to materialism, the latter are unable to consider rationally evidences for an original creative act, no less intermittent creative acts, in the evolutionary development of the universe.

But how does such closed-mindedness square with an ultimate concern for objectivity and truth? If one shuts the door *a priori* to any evidence or theory which does not fit in with his metaphysical world view, it is difficult to see how that person or his position can be seen as a champion of truth, objectivity, or freedom of thought. No doubt some of the recalcitrance to nonnaturalistic ideas in cosmology and biology are due to the naive literalism and reactionary propaganda espoused by certain fundamentalists. But such views are off the mainstream of Christian thought. The bottom line is that the Christian need not be committed prior to an examination of the evidence to any particular scientific theory, although some may fit in better than others with his Bible and his creed. But however difficult it may appear to harmonize a particular, tentatively held scientific theory with his religious beliefs, intellectually, he need not fear any ultimate contradiction because he has confidence in the truthfulness of the God who revealed himself not only in Scripture and creed, but also in nature. He can, then, approach his task as scientist with confidence and a mind open to facts from whatever source they arise.

Christianity, then, is no less open to revision of its beliefs than any other system. Surely, there are some unrevisable postulates, *e.g.*, the existence of God, the Trinity, the incarnation and saving work of Christ, etc. To give up on these is simply to give up on Christianity. But other positions have their unrevisable postulates, and they are no fewer than those of Christians, for they must assert the negation of each postulate held by Christians. Each world view has, then, the same number of unrevisable postulates. Consequently, no one is more closed to revision than the other on the metaphysical level. As I have argued, however, it seems that naturalism is less flexible on the scientific level.

By now it should be clear that Christianity is no more incompatible with the stated objectives of a liberal arts education than any of the alternatives. This is not to say that a liberal arts education must be Christian, merely that it can be.

III

Finally, it remains to be shown that a Christian Studies Program is not merely not inconsistent with the liberal arts, but that there is actually an inherent compatibility between them. Only a sketch of such an argument can be presented given present spatial constraints. I shall attempt to accomplish this by showing how the basic metaphysical presuppositions common to all expressions of Christian theism actually lend support to and provide an intellectual foundation for the pursuit of liberal learning. These presuppositions are: (1) the existence of an eternal, morally and rationally perfect, and personal God, and (2) man as a being created in the image of this God.

That such a God as Christians believe in is capable of grounding the liberal arts in an adequately founded system of thought should be evident from the fact that, even during the so-called "Age of Faith," the liberal arts were an integral part of university education and a necessary preparation for the priesthood. The God of Christian theism is a God of reason and moral perfection. His *logos* is co-eternal with his being. Indeed, as the early fathers argued, how could God the Father ever be without his eternal *logos*, for Christians, God the Son? Moreover, the *logos* of God is the creative agent through whom the heavens and the earth have been made, and, therefore, the latter must be organized in accordance with and expressive of the orderly, rational, and consistent nature of that *logos*. The world must be a cosmos, a system capable of predictability and manipulation by creatures endowed with the capacity to abstract and plan. Creation itself is fundamentally good and worthy of attention and, therefore, the investigation of the liberal arts as well as the sciences is not only a possible enterprise for man, but one which he has an imperative to pursue.

In addition, belief in such a God forces upon man the recognition of his own limitations not only physically and mentally, but also morally. A perfectly moral God will create a world which is consistent with his own moral nature, and the society of men will not be free to do whatsoever they please, but will be obliged to treat their world, their neighbor, and themselves in a manner that will do justice to the love, goodness, and integrity of God himself. Belief in this sort of an origin to the universe will require of man that he establish societies which guarantee justice and equality of opportunity to all and which demand that all persons be treated as persons. Moreover, intellectual pursuits will be directed by a requirement for truth no matter how unpalatable, a condition absolutely essential for any truly rational study of the cosmos.

In addition, such a God grounds reality in a person, and personality, instead of being a happy epiphenomenon riding blissfully but precariously on the waves of an ever-predominant and eventually resurgent meaningless movement of molecules, will be seen as the crown of the universe, a priceless treasure that must be treated with the most delicate respect and honor. It is indeed ironic than man, having reached the technical and theoretical heights of the twentieth century, can best picture his mental superior from outer space as a blend of Kermit the Frog and Alfred E. Newman. Surely, even the most average human specimen is a more attractive alternative, but compared with the vision of man expressed by Michaelangelo's *David* or any of the great Greek statues of antiquity, man's coming to see himself as a little lower than E. T. is surely a tragedy of epic proportions.

Given the biblical vision of man, he has indeed a noble purpose and his life, regardless of individual limitations, is given a transcendent value that no mere utilitarian conception can come close to approaching in depth or vitality. The aims and ends of human life cease, when viewed in this perspective, to see in happiness or personal success the ultimate measuring stick of importance, value or usefulness. Man, as a person created in the image of God, has importance as an individual, regardless of his accomplishments or lack thereof. His function is to glorify God and enjoy Him for all time. How and in what circumstances the individual does this is relatively unimportant. The vital question concerns the personal interrelationship which one has with his God and the extent to which that relationship has become visible through his person and activity.

In this connection, mention should also be made of the Christian doctrine of the Fall. Although both Christianity and Judaism teach that man was created in God's image, they also hold that that image has been tarnished by man's willful rebellion against the sovereignty and goodness of God. Having fallen into this wretched state, he is not to be trusted. Such a view of man is not, however, either pessimistic or mythical. Since man is redeemable, it is not pessimistic; since man truly is prone to hubris and self-worship, it is realistic. Indeed, it is those times in Western history when men have considered themselves capable of overcoming the inherent limitations of human autonomy by dint of their spirituality or their rationality that the mass of mankind has had to suffer under the most oppressive and violent outbursts of human inhumanity to both man and nature. A healthy doctrine of original sin leads to a healthy mistrust of our fellow human and a consequent balance of power insured by our continual vigilance over the social order.

Lastly, the Christian view of eschatology gives to human endeavor, including, indeed especially, the liberal arts, a transcendent value and consequent purpose without which the final outcome can only be intellectual despair and emotional despondency. That God is the end as well as the beginning of all things is a necessary postulate of Christian theism, and, I believe, one which gives human history as well as individual human lives ultimate purpose, meaning, and hope.

In conclusion, the Christian Studies Program ought to be viewed as a "research program" in the liberal arts, and one which possesses a grand intellectual heritage and tremendous intellectual strength. Indeed, it is that tradition which is largely responsible for preserving our past and developing both within and from that past the magnificent legacy in which all of us share and to the continuance of which all of us are committed. Given the understanding of Christianity and the Christian Studies Program outlined above, it would appear an inescapable conclusion that such a world view is at least as compatible with the liberal arts as any other, and that in many respects it offers possibilities far superior to those of any of its rivals.

Index